Darkness Receding

Darkness Receding

Biblical Hermeneutics, Depression, and Pastoral Care

MARION L. S. CARSON

CASCADE *Books* • Eugene, Oregon

DARKNESS RECEDING
Biblical Hermeneutics, Depression, and Pastoral Care

Cascade Books
An Imprint of Wipf and Stock Publishers
199 W. 8th Ave., Suite 3
Eugene, OR 97401

www.wipfandstock.com

PAPERBACK ISBN: 978-1-6667-5683-8
HARDCOVER ISBN: 978-1-6667-5684-5
EBOOK ISBN: 978-1-6667-5685-2

Cataloguing-in-Publication data:

Names: Carson, Marion L. S., author.

Title: Darkness receding : biblical hermeneutics, depression, and pastoral care / Marion L. S. Carson.

Description: Eugene, OR: Cascade Books, 2026. | Includes bibliographical references.

Identifiers: ISBN 978-1-6667-5683-8 (paperback). | ISBN 978-1-6667-5684-5 (hardcover). | ISBN 978-1-6667-5685-2 (ebook).

Subjects: LCSH: Pastoral care. | Pastoral theology. | Pastoral psychology. | Depression, Mental—Religious aspects—Christianity.

Classification: BV4011 C36 2026 (print). | BV4011. (epub).

02/20/26

In memory of my parents

Contents

Acknowledgments

This book is dedicated to the memory of my beloved parents, Charles and Jessie Johnstone, who did their utmost to provide a loving environment in which to grow and learn. Douglas, my husband, has been consistently supportive and encouraging throughout the years it has taken to complete this book. I am indebted to Dr. Nicola Watt for scrutinizing my writing on the medical aspects of depression. I am also grateful to Dr. Jonathan Wilson for taking the time to read a draft of the manuscript and for his encouragement of the project. An anonymous reviewer at Wipf and Stock gave invaluable feedback, which rescued me from losing exegetical focus in the chapters on Paul. I am grateful too, for the opportunity at various stages to present aspects of this book at New College, Edinburgh, Charles University in Prague, and at the Society of Biblical Literature Biblical Studies and Spiritual Care Unit. To all who have been influential, thank you. Any inaccuracies and errors are, of course, entirely my responsibility.

Abbreviations

ACCS	Ancient Christian Commentary on Scripture
AJP	*American Journal of Psychiatry*
AThR	*Anglican Theological Review*
BTB	*Biblical Theology Bulletin*
DN	*The Dark Night of the Soul.* In *The Collected Works of St John of the Cross*, translated by Kieran Kavanaugh and Otilio Rodriguez, 353–457. Washington, DC: ICS, 1991
ESV	English Standard Version
EvQ	*Evangelical Quarterly*
IBC	Interpretation: A Bible Commentary for Teaching and Preaching
Int	*Interpretation*
JRE	*Journal of Religious Ethics*
JSNT	*Journal for the Study of the New Testament*
JSNTSup	Journal for the Study of the New Testament Supplement Series
KJV	King James Version
LCC	Library of Christian Classics
LNTS	Library of New Testament Studies
NICNT	New International Commentary on the New Testament
NIV	New International Version
NRSV	New Revised Standard Version

NTAbh	Neutestamentliche Abhandlungen
NTL	New Testament Library
SBL	Society of Biblical Literature
SymS	Symposium Series
SemeiaSt	Semeia Studies
STI	Studies in Theological Interpretation
TDNT	*Theological Dictionary of the New Testament*. Edited by Gerhard Kittel and Gerhard Friedrich. Translated by Geoffrey W. Bromiley. 10 vols. Grand Rapids: Eerdmans, 1964–1976
TS	*Theological Studies*
WBC	Word Biblical Commentary
WUNT	Wissenschaftliche Untersuchungen zum Neuen Testament
ZNW	*Zeitschrift für die neutestamentliche Wissenschaft und die Kunde der älteren Kirche*

1

Introduction

Whoever, then, thinks that he understands the Holy Scriptures, or any part of them, but puts such an interpretation upon them as does not tend to build up this twofold love of God and our neighbor, does not yet understand them as he ought.

—*Augustine, De Doctrina Christiana 1.36.40*

THE BIBLE AND THE PASTORAL CARE OF PEOPLE WITH MENTAL HEALTH CHALLENGES

The question of how the Bible can inform the pastoral care of people with mental health challenges is an important one for people engaged in pastoral ministry. Yet it is largely neglected by pastoral theologians, and is rarely the subject of in-depth exploration in seminaries and universities. John Swinton notes this lack in his recent book *Finding Jesus in the Storm: The Spiritual Lives of People with Mental Health Challenges*. "Learning the skill of using Scripture pastorally," he says, "is a vital aspect of ministry that is not always given the consideration it deserves." Given that the Bible is normative for all Christian traditions, and the book to which many if not most Christians will turn to for comfort, there is, as Swinton says, a need for biblical interpretation that will bring healing to those with mental health challenges.[1] In this book it is my intention to try to address this need, in the hope that it will contribute to the as yet small but increasing amount of literature on the subject.

The lack of scholarly work on the Bible and pastoral care of mental health challenges is part of a wider problem with regard to the use of Scripture in pastoral care in general. In large part, this is due to the difficulties of engaging in interdisciplinary studies. In universities and seminaries alike, biblical studies has been taught alongside pastoral theology but without much, if any, attempt at integration. This stems, to a large extent, from the dominance of the historical-critical method in biblical studies throughout much of the twentieth century. Students have been taught to view the text as a historical document that can tell us about the nature and beliefs of the early church, but much less about how these texts might be relevant to our everyday contemporary lives. As Stephen Pattison says,

> This minute, historical, critical and analytical perspective has yielded many benefits, but it also has had the effect of making it very difficult to integrate specific textual insights with broad theological concerns, or with Christian life in general.[2]

As Pattison notes, the complexities of the results of the historical-critical method have led many involved in pastoral ministry to wonder if and how the documents contained in the Bible can be considered relevant for use in pastoral care at all. And unfortunately, this has meant that the numbers of writers who appreciate the need for using the Bible in an informed way in pastoral care tend to be few.[3]

The problem has been compounded by the fact that in the mid-twentieth century, many writers began to focus on pastoral counseling as the most effective tool for those engaged in pastoral care. As a result, counseling skills and the psychological theories that underpinned them became the main resources for use in the pastoral setting.[4] Some, such as Donald Capps and Howard Clinebell, drew on developmental psychology

1. Swinton, *Finding Jesus in the Storm*, 101.

2. Pattison, *Critique*, 106.

3. For an overview of the use of the Bible in writings on pastoral care, see Ballard "Use of Scripture."

4. Clinebell, *Basic Types of Pastoral Care*; Jacobs, *Still Small Voice*; see Narramore, *Psychology of Counseling*. For an account of the history of the pastoral counseling movement in America, see Townsend, "Pastoral Counseling's History."

to advance theories of pastoral care.[5] However, the use of psychology drew the criticism, particularly from conservative evangelical writers on pastoral care, that spiritual matters were being marginalized, that the moral aspect of Christian life was being ignored, and that the voice of Scripture was being excluded. In fact, some objected strongly to the use of secular psychology at all, believing the Bible to be the *only* resource the Christian counselor should use.[6] Others who are friendlier towards psychology and psychiatry have been willing to incorporate these ideas while continuing to see the Bible as the primary source on which practitioners should draw.[7] Nevertheless, it must be said that the temptation for many writers on pastoral counseling has been to see the Bible as a source of spiritual medicine that is to be dispensed and applied as appropriate.[8] Indeed, the tendency among many, if not most, writers on pastoral care has been towards proof-texting, or using the Bible to give spiritual legitimacy to the psychological approach being taken. In many of these writings there is a neglect, and in some a suspicion, of the insights of biblical scholarship, with the result that the Bible tends to be used in a superficial and simplistic way.

OPENING UP THE WAY

Thankfully, an increasing interest in hermeneutics is helping to address this problem.[9] The gulf between biblical studies and practical theology is slowly beginning to narrow. There is a growing recognition that different hermeneutical approaches enable us to allow the biblical texts to speak into diverse reading situations.[10] Feminist, liberation, and cross-cultural hermeneutics (among others) have highlighted the dangers inherent in simply applying Scripture directly to contemporary situations without consideration of the

5. Capps, *Decades of Life*; Capps, *Still Growing.*

6. This is the general approach taken by practitioners of "biblical counseling." See Powlison, *Biblical Counseling Movement*; Shields and Bredfeldt, *Caring for Souls.*

7. See, for example, Collins, *Christian Counseling*; Hurding, *Roots and Shoots.*

8. Carson, "Deep Heat and Bandages?"

9. On the need for a hermeneutic for pastoral intervention see, for example, Schultz, "Responsible Hermeneutics for Wisdom Literature"; Maier and Monroe "Biblical Hermeneutics and Christian Psychology." See further Briggs, "Biblical Hermeneutics and Practical Theology."

10. Thiselton, *New Horizons in Hermeneutics*, 558.

experience and context of the contemporary reader.[11] The development of canonical approaches to Scripture has better enabled scholarship to take a holistic rather than an atomizing view of the biblical literature.[12] In other words, we now have a wealth of scholarship on which to draw, which can help us both to understand the texts in their historical context and to be able to relate them to various contexts today. It is pleasing to note that some biblical scholars are beginning to ask questions as to how these ancient texts might be able to address contemporary pastoral issues, for example, in the areas of disability and bereavement.[13] Recently, too, a growing number of practical and pastoral theologians has begun to discuss the place of the biblical text within their discipline.[14] With regard to mental health, by far the most interest is among biblical scholars who see the Bible as containing "trauma texts," which provide rich resources for those working with victims of torture, exile, and disaster.[15] Nevertheless, scholarly works that focus on the Bible and mental health in general remain few.[16]

Focusing on Depression

The task of integrating research on biblical studies, mental health and pastoral care is, to say the least, daunting. We need to be mindful of the varied and complex nature of the biblical literature itself, of our own hermeneutical assumptions, and of the experience and context of the people we are

11. As an introduction, see the collection of essays edited by Gorman, *Scripture and Its Interpretation.*

12. See Childs, *Biblical Theology of the Old and New Testaments.*

13. Examples include Hopkins and Koppel, *Grounded in the Living Word*; Macaskill, *Autism and the Church*; Melcher et al., *Bible and Disability*; Bennet and Rowland, *In a Glass Darkly*; Brueggemann, "Formfulness of Grief."

14. Ballard and Holmes, *Bible in Pastoral Practice*; Oliver, *Holy Bible, Human Bible*; Pattison et al., *Using the Bible in Christian Ministry*; Cartledge, "Use of Scripture in Practical Theology"; Bennett, *Using the Bible in Practical Theology.* And see the collection of papers in "The Bible as Pastor," a special issue of *Contact: Practical Theology and Pastoral Care* (150.1) from 2006, edited by Paul Ballard. The same journal is now called *Practical Theology.*

15. See, for example, Boase and Frechette, *Bible Through the Lens of Trauma*; Kotrosits and Taussig, *Re-reading the Gospel of Mark*; Lee and Mandolfo, *Lamentations in Ancient and Contemporary Cultural Contexts.*

16. See, however, the recent collection of essays in Cook and Hamley, *Bible and Mental Health*; also Lawrence, *Bible and Bedlam*; Mainwaring, *Mark, Mutuality and Mental Health*; Capps, *Jesus, the Village Psychiatrist.*

seeking to serve. And if the biblical literature is complex, so too is mental illness. Mental health challenges take many forms, and individuals' experiences and understandings of them are also very varied. A trauma-informed hermeneutic may be helpful for someone who is suffering from post-traumatic stress disorder, for example, but not for someone who is experiencing psychosis. Just as we have to understand the text of the Scriptures, we also have to try to understand the texts of our "living human documents."[17]

Given all these complexities, it is wise for us to impose some limitations on our study. With regard to mental health, we will limit our discussion to one particular area—severe depression. There are several reasons for this choice. The first is its prevalence. Depression is said to be the most common type of mental illness and is often called the "common cold" of psychiatry. According to the World Health Organization approximately 280 million people around the world suffer from depression.[18] Millions of dollars are spent on its treatment each year, and many hours of work are lost because of it. The prevalence of depression in Western society as a whole is also reflected in our churches, and pastors are bound to come up against it sooner or later. The need for pastors to understand the nature of depression and how to be able to help those who suffer from it is an urgent, major concern.

The second reason for focusing on severe depression is its very serious nature. Depressive illness can result in people being unable to work, and can cause serious problems within families and relationships. It can also be fatal. In his book *Darkness Visible*, William Styron gives a searing account of his experience:

> Depression is a disorder of mood, so mysteriously painful and elusive in the way that it becomes known to the self—the mediating intellect—as to verge close to being beyond description. It thus remains nearly incomprehensible to those who have not experienced it in its extreme mode.[19]

As Styron notes, it is all but impossible for those who have not had such a painful experience of severe depression to understand what sufferers are going through. His description forces us to make the distinction between

17. Gerkin, *Living Human Document*.

18. See World Health Organization, "Depressive Disorder (Depression)." See further Hasin et al., "Epidemiology of Depressive Disorders."

19. Styron, *Darkness Visible*, 7.

depression as a severe clinical illness and our everyday notions of being "fed up" or a bit down.

Third, for the Christian, depression can bring about spiritual problems as well as psychological and physical suffering. An experience of severe depression can give rise to questioning all that one believes. In particular, many people speak of a loss of hope, which robs them not only of a sense of a future but of meaningfulness in their everyday lives in the present. Diminishing faith and hope can be compounded by growing guilt and shame—especially if the individual is part of a community in which doubt and questioning are hardly tolerated.

Clearly, then, there are profound pastoral needs in this area, and pastors can be left feeling helpless and in need of guidance. And yet, as Donald Capps says, pastoral carers are called to be "agents of hope" in the church.[20] So how can we be so for people who are feeling hopeless? And how can the Bible help us to do this?

Romans 5:1–5 on Suffering and Hope

Our second limitation has to do with the use of the biblical literature. In order to explore how Scripture can inform our pastoral practice, I have chosen one passage as a test case. Since we are concerned with the loss of hope in depression, I have chosen to examine Rom 5:1–5, in which Paul spells out his view of the relationship between suffering and hope for believers. Christians rejoice in suffering, he says, because they know they are justified in Christ. Rooted in faith, perseverance in suffering will eventually lead to hope. Paul was writing these words to a young, vulnerable church in a hostile environment, with the aim of encouraging them to keep going in difficult circumstances. How might Paul's words help us to care for people who have, because of illness (namely severe depression), become unable to hold on to hope?

Hermeneutics: The Influence of Foundationalism

This brings us to the last limitation we must impose on our study. In order to find out how this passage might inform the pastoral care of people suffering from severe depression, we will use the insights of character (or

20. Capps, *Agents of Hope.*

virtue) ethics to help us understand what the passage might be saying to us today. Why? I have already noted that some writers on pastoral care tend to understand the Bible as though it were a medicine cabinet: applying its propositions and instructions is all that is needed to help us through the difficulties of life. The aim of reading is to find out what needs to be done in order to alleviate the problem. This way of approaching Scripture is not confined to writers on pastoral care. In fact, in my experience it tends to be the default hermeneutic of many "ordinary" readers of Scripture, who in their daily devotions look to the text to provide them with emotional comfort and moral instruction.[21]

This view of Scripture stems from a hermeneutical standpoint that we might call foundationalism—the belief that human beings can reach a knowledge and understanding of "objective truth." In their book, *Beyond Foundationalism*, Grenz and Franke write:

> The goal of the foundationalist agenda is the discovery of an approach to knowledge that will provide rational human beings with absolute, incontestable certainty regarding the truthfulness of their beliefs. According to foundationalists, the acquisition of knowledge ought to proceed in a manner somewhat similar to the construction of a building. Knowledge must be built on a sure foundation. The Enlightenment epistemological foundation consists on a set of incontestable beliefs or unassailable first principles on the basis of which the pursuit of knowledge can proceed. These basic beliefs or first principles must be universal, objective, and discernible to any rational person.[22]

The assumption in Grenz and Franke's account of foundationalism is that the search for knowledge can be undertaken with scientific objectivity.[23] This, of course, was the assumption of the scientific method, which gained ascendency in the Enlightenment period. As far as biblical studies was concerned, this assumption led to the belief that if the exact meaning of each word and idiom could be found, and the historical context of the text understood, then the original meaning of the text could be discovered.

This had two main consequences. First, so-called liberal thinkers looked to the Bible to provide an account of the religious experience of the

21. By "ordinary" I mean Christians who have little or no theological education. See Astley, *Ordinary Theology*, 56.

22. Grenz and Franke, *Beyond Foundationalism*, 23.

23. For the critique that Grenz and Franke are working with only one aspect of foundationalism (the Cartesian), see Bergmann, "Foundationalism."

communities represented within it, and conservatives looked to the Bible to provide divine revelation.[24] Scripture was mined for facts and data, whether as a record of the experience of its writers, or as the direct word of God to his people. Second, given this view of Scripture, it was natural for Christians to look to it for guidance for how they should live. Since Enlightenment ethical theory focused on decision-making, readers of Scripture tended to approach it with the question, "What ought I to do?" in mind. Consequently, many came to see the Bible as a book of instruction whose function was to provide the basis of individual moral lives. And as we have seen, this foundationalist approach continues to influence a good deal of thinking on how the Bible should inform pastoral care.

CHARACTER ETHICS AS A HERMENEUTICAL LENS

In recent years, foundationalism has become discredited.[25] There is a growing appreciation that our ability to amass knowledge will always be constrained by our cultural context and by our experience and human weakness. Amos Yong writes,

> The human capacity for knowing is not only circumscribed by cultural context, but also limited by sin and the fall. As such, there is neither an Archimedean vantage point of knowledge, nor is there a sturdy foundation underneath. All knowledge is undeniably tradition dependent.[26]

That is to say, we need to recognize that people see and understand things from different perspectives, and that we cling to the belief that human endeavor can bring about absolute certainty at our peril.

With regard to ethics, a change has also taken place. Many scholars now argue that it takes more than obedience to rules to enable us to live good and happy lives. An emphasis on compliance and personal rectitude has given way to an interest in the place of character and the virtues in the development of flourishing communities.[27] In Protestant theology, the work of Stanley Hauerwas has been deeply influential in moving the focus

24. See Murphy, *Beyond Liberalism and Fundamentalism*, 11–35; Grenz and Franke, *Beyond Foundationalism*, 57–92.

25. See, for example, Yong, *Dialogical Spirit*, 19–46.

26. Yong, *Dialogical Spirit*, 23.

27. See, for example, Jones, *Transformed Judgment*; Meilaender, *Theory and Practice of Virtue*; Porter, *Recovery of Virtue*.

away from the piety and obedience of individuals to the development of Christian "communities of character," in which our participation in the story of Christ's rule informs our lives together.[28] In contrast to deontological and utilitarian approaches to ethics, character ethics holds that it is not enough to think about what we ought to be doing; we also have to be able to say what kind of people we need to be. Further, rather than focusing on the rights and wrongs of individuals' behavior, character ethics turns its attention to traits we need to have in order to flourish in healthy communities. These characteristics are known as virtues, habits of mind such as patience, tolerance, and perseverance, which are essential for helping us build healthy societies. The way to learn about these habits of mind is through the telling and reading of stories in which the accrued wisdom of communities is preserved and transmitted over generations.

Character (or virtue) ethics has gained ground in many other walks of life besides ethics—from philosophy to education and business, to medicine, nursing and psychology.[29] Of particular importance for the field of mental health is so-called positive psychology, which argues that the virtues can be the basis for happiness and well-being and, indeed, a defense against mental illness.[30] It has also made its mark among biblical scholars who wish to avoid the trap of seeing biblical ethics solely in terms of rules and prescriptions. According to Lisa Sowle Cahill,

> In a framework of character ethics in which 'character' indicates a process of communal formation of individual identity, the Bible does not necessarily have to produce specific moral rules in order to be authoritative. Rather, it orients Christian persons and communities around general values, principles, or virtues that reflect God's self-disclosure in Christ. Central among these are, for example, repentance, love of neighbor, self-sacrifice, cross bearing, forgiveness, nonviolence (closer to a moral rule), and compassion.[31]

28. Hauerwas, *Community of Character*, 96.

29. See, for example, Peterson and Seligman, *Character Strengths and Virtues*; Radden and Sadler, *Virtuous Psychiatrist*.

30. Seligman, "Positive Psychology," 4: "We have discovered that there are human strengths that act as buffers against mental illness: courage, future-mindedness, optimism, interpersonal skill, faith, work ethic, hope, honesty, perseverance, the capacity for flow and insight, to name several." See further Hart, *Positive Psychology*.

31. Cahill, "Christian Character," 10. Other recent studies taking this approach include Esler, "Social Identity."

Scholars who view Scripture through the lens of character ethics want to see how it can inform the lives of people who wish to embody the story of Scripture in their communities.[32] This must surely include the practice of pastoral care, which is a vital part of the task of building communities of character.[33]

All these developments offer real opportunities for the integration of biblical studies and pastoral theology. The task is made easier by an increasing interest in narrative on the part of both biblical scholars and pastoral theologians. Literary criticism and narrative theory have drawn attention to the biblical text as the story of God's intervention in history and to the stories of those who wrestle with the understanding of being his people.[34] Pastoral theologians, too, have become more aware of the value of narrative and wisdom in the pastoral care relationship.[35] These developments open the way for interdisciplinary exploration of the relationship between God and his people, and his people with one another.[36]

OUTLINE OF THE BOOK

In this book then, I propose to ask how Paul's words in Rom 5:1–5 might inform the pastoral care of people suffering from severe depression, using the hermeneutical lens provided by character ethics. How can these words help pastoral carers to be agents of hope to those who feel hopeless? Before we explore the biblical text, however, our first task will be to provide some understanding of the nature of depression. This will be done in chapter 2. I shall begin by explaining it in clinical terms so that readers can see how depression is currently understood in psychiatry, the approach that dominates contemporary discussions. Then I shall present some literary accounts to help pastoral carers to understand more of people's *experiences* of depression, including those who have a Christian faith. These literary accounts highlight the sense of hopelessness that often accompanies depression and the spiritual problems which can compound the suffering.

32. See, for example, Fowl and Jones, *Reading in Communion*.

33. Messer, *SCM Study Guide*, 191–92. See Hauerwas and Willimon, *Resident Aliens*, chapters 6 and 7.

34. See Rogerson "Gifts and Challenges"; and Bartholomew, "In Front of the Text."

35. See Anderson, "Bible and Pastoral Care."

36. Ballard and Holmes, "General Introduction," xv.

Chapter 3 will offer an initial exploration of Rom 5:1–5 along traditional lines, using a historical-critical approach to the text. It will also adopt a foundationalist hermeneutic, asking how this passage can inform the pastoral care of people suffering from depression. I shall suggest that approaching the text with the question, "What ought I to do?" in mind entails certain problems for our efforts to help people who are suffering from depression, and that an alternative hermeneutical lens might prove more fruitful. In chapter 4, character ethics will be introduced as an alternative hermeneutical lens. Hauerwas's belief that all believers have a part to play in the story of the kingdom will be central to the study. I shall show that ideas of community, narrative, and the virtues are to be found in Paul, and provide an explanation of the virtues as "distinctive excellences" necessary for flourishing communities.

In chapters 5–7, we will revisit Rom 5:1–5 and conduct an in-depth exploration using the lens of character ethics. We will explore the idea of faith as a virtue and, drawing on recent developments in Pauline studies, broaden our understanding of the concept of faith and trust to include faithfulness in imitation of the faithfulness of Christ himself. We will ask how it is that faith can help us to rejoice and persevere in the suffering that is an inevitable and indeed a crucial part of the experience of the Christian journey. In chapter 6, the sequence of thought in Rom 5:3–4 will be reexamined, focusing on the ideas of perseverance, character, and hope. The guiding hermeneutical question will be "What kind of people does God want us to be?" rather than "What ought I to do?" We will see that Christians are hopeful people because God has given them the gifts of faith and hope. Chapter 7 will focus on the third theological virtue, *agapē* love, as the means of expressing faith and hope (Rom 5:5).

In chapter 8, making use of a case study, we will undertake a comparison of the pastoral implications of both interpretations of Rom 5:1–5 and argue that the hermeneutic adopted with regard to the Bible has a direct impact on how the Bible is used in pastoral care, and indeed on how pastoral care itself is understood. I shall suggest that a foundationalist hermeneutic tends to result in a didactic and corrective approach to pastoral care whereas an interpretation informed by character ethics encourages a more compassionate and egalitarian view of the pastoral role.

Chapter 9 will build upon these findings and continue the theme of practical pastoral care of people with depression. The Christian story has continued over centuries, and as believers have participated in that story, learning how to be faithful, hopeful, and loving people, much wisdom has been accrued. Drawing on this wisdom, we will note that liturgy, art, and music can be invaluable in pastoral care, and that the traditions of acedia and the dark night of the soul can help us have a more nuanced view of spiritual distress than we often encounter in our churches today. I shall suggest that the wisdom contained in traditions such as these can teach us a great deal about how to develop communities of character in which the stigma and (potentially) the incidence of severe depression can be reduced. Chapter 10 will turn to the broader question of how the Bible can be used in the pastoral care of people suffering from depression in particular and from mental health challenges in general. It will offer a critique of the work of Jay Adams and Larry Crabb, both foundationalist readers of Scripture, and outline the advantages of a hermeneutic guided by character ethics as a biblically informed approach to pastoral care.

A Brief Note on Hope

Throughout our study the notion of hope will be crucial. But what is it we are talking about when we refer to hope?[37] What does it mean to say that someone is hopeful or hopeless? In psychological terms, the person who is hopeful is able to see that things can be better than they are now. They have the desire for something to happen which will bring this about and the expectation that it is realizable. For example, a woman who is physically ill may have both the desire to be well and the expectation that medical treatment will make this possible; her hope is a response to the difficult situation in which she finds herself. To hope in this sense then is to be more than optimistic—it is to be able to envisage a better time and to be able to cooperate in bringing it about. In the case of severe depression, it is this ability which is compromised. The clinically depressed person cannot imagine a better time, and does not have the ability or inclination to help change things—there is simply no point in doing so. The loss of hope that is characteristic of depression, then, is not merely the loss of optimism, or the fading of a desire for things (for example, money or possessions), but

37. In fact, it is very hard to pin down what hope as a concept means. As John Macquarrie (*In Search of Humanity*, 243) notes: "Hope is a diffuse, inclusive concept, denoting a mood or an attitude in which beliefs, emotions, imagination and purpose are all combined . . . characterised by a measure of confidence and affirmative expectation about the future."

the loss of the ability to perceive that things can change for the better.[38] As Ratcliffe puts it, it is the loss of the ability to see that "significant possibilities can be actualized."[39] Such a loss constitutes an existential threat to the sufferer, and it is for this reason that depression can be life-threatening.

In the life of the believer, however, there is another element to this characteristic loss of hope. According to John Webster, a hopeful Christian is one who

> knows in faith that in the economy of God's grace, enacted in the resurrection of Jesus and the giving of the Spirit, and lived out in the company of the saints, his or her future is secure; and so the Christian who hopes is one who turns to that future and acts in its light, confident because in the Spirit, Jesus Christ is our present help and pledge of our coming consummation.[40]

If a Christian loses the capacity to hope, then, he or she loses the ability not only to see that the future is secure but also to see that Jesus Christ is the present help and pledge. In other words, that hopelessness robs him or her of the deep certainties of the faith, which have been the mainstay of Christian identity. The person can no longer see God at work in the world, let alone that there can be "resurrection from life's failures and defeats" or the "power of the rebirth of life out of the shadows of death."[41] From a pastoral point of view, the loss of this hope is a dimension of the experience of depression that cannot be ignored. For in the life of the believer such hopelessness is not merely the loss of an ability to put one foot in front of the other—it is the loss of all that has previously given meaning to life, both as an individual and as part of a community. How Christian pastoral carers can be biblically informed agents of hope in such an agonizing situation is a major concern of this book.

38. On the differences between hope as desire or optimism see Pruyser, "Maintaining Hope in Adversity."

39. Ratcliffe, *Experiences of Depression*, 110.

40. Webster, "Hope."

41. Moltmann, *In the End—The Beginning*, 1.

2

Depression: Medical, Personal, and Spiritual Perspectives

No worst, there is none. Pitched past pitch of grief,
More pangs will, schooled at forepangs, wilder wring.
Comforter, where, where is your comforting?
—*Gerard Manley Hopkins*

INTRODUCTION

Before we can discuss how, if at all, Paul's statement in Rom 5:1–5 might inform the pastoral care of people suffering from severe depression, we need to have some understanding of the nature of the disorder and how it is currently treated. In Western societies, depression is managed by medical professionals, psychologists, and counselors. Someone who is experiencing extreme low mood is likely to consult a medical doctor who will prescribe medication and perhaps refer him or her to a counselor or psychotherapist. For those involved in pastoral care, it is helpful to know something of the approach these professionals take and the treatments currently on offer. We will see, however, that knowledge of the medical approach to depression, while useful, is of limited value in the pastoral setting. It is not enough to know the signs and symptoms of depression—we must also be able to try to draw alongside those who suffer in this way, and where possible, accompany them on their journey with sensitivity and wisdom. In order to be able to do that it is essential to have some understanding of the *experience* of those for whom we are caring. The purpose of this chapter therefore is to explore the nature of depression, its medical diagnosis and treatment, and to gain further insights from personal accounts which might help us understand the nature of depression at a deeper level.

WHAT IS DEPRESSION?

We are inclined to misuse the term "depression" in everyday conversation. We speak of feeling depressed when we feel fed up, disappointed, or a bit low. Such misuse of the term is galling to those for whom severe depression is a reality. In his personal memoir of the experience of severe depression, *Darkness Visible*, the novelist William Styron angrily declares that the word has "slithered through the language like a slug, leaving little trace of its intrinsic malevolence and preventing by its very insipidity, a general awareness of the horrible intensity of the disease when out of control."[1]

The point is that there is a world of difference between the experience of feeling "low" or "down" (which is a normal part of life) and a severe clinical depression, and we need to be careful of the language we use. Severe depression is quite different from everyday emotional upheavals. It is a debilitating, even dangerous medical condition that has discernible characteristics and patterns.

Of course, it takes a clinician to determine what should be deemed clinical depression, and it is helpful for us to have some idea of the criteria on which this is medically diagnosed. Modern psychiatry recognizes that there are different kinds of depression and many causes. For example, there is the depression that is part and parcel of bipolar disorder (formerly known as manic-depressive psychosis). The person experiences periods of extreme low mood, as well as episodes of mania, in which there is a sense of intense euphoria. These states can last for periods of days or weeks. Or, there is postnatal depression, in which, following childbirth, a woman experiences an incapacitating low mood, which can often result in her inability to care for her child. Depression can come about as a result of illnesses such as glandular fever or thyroid problems, or from organic changes in the brain, such as a tumor, or dementia.

1. Styron, *Darkness Visible*, 37.

These instances of depression are known to have specific causes, namely, biochemical or physical changes in the brain. However, the majority of people who are diagnosed with depression today do not have any of these conditions. In other words, for most people, there is no identifiable physical cause for their extreme sadness and pain. For some, there may be a genetic component to their illness: bipolar disorder is known to have a genetic cause, and a tendency toward low mood can run in families. However, for many, no such familial pattern can be observed. Some may be able to point to a particular event that seemed to be the beginning or cause of the downward spiral. Some may attribute their depression to something that happened in childhood, or to serious loss or disappointment in adulthood. Others, however, can become depressed for no apparent reason, and are unable to identify any specific incident as the cause or starting point.

How Doctors Diagnose Depression

It is the job of the doctor to try to find out what the root of the problem is, for this will determine the kind of treatment to be prescribed. In Western medical practice, the clinician will look for a particular set of signs and symptoms which together suggest that what the patient is describing is recognized as a clinical depression. At present, there are two main sources doctors consult to help them in their diagnosis.[2] The best known is the *Diagnostic and Statistical Manual of Mental Disorders* (*DSM*), which is produced by the American Psychiatric Association. It is concerned only with psychiatric disorders, and is used throughout the United States and beyond. It has gone through numerous changes and developments and is now in its fifth incarnation—the *DSM-5*.[3] The second source is the *ICD-11* which is produced by the World Health Organization.[4] The *ICD-11* is used in Great Britain and Europe, although the *DSM* is also consulted by clinicians and frequently cited in British writing about psychiatry.

In the *DSM-5*, in order for a major depressive episode to be diagnosed, five or more of the following must be reported or observed over a period of two weeks:

2. Understanding of the nature and treatment of what is now known as depression has changed over history. See Lawlor, *From Melancholia to Prozac*; Tacchi and Scott, *Depression*.

3. American Psychiatric Association, *Diagnostic and Statistical Manual*.

4. World Health Organization, *ICD-11 International Classification of Diseases*.

- low mood
- diminished interest or pleasure in activities
- weight loss or weight gain
- inability to sleep or sleeping too much
- slowing down physically
- fatigue
- feelings of worthlessness or guilt
- poor concentration
- recurrent thoughts of death or suicide

As well as low mood, the ICD -11 lists the following:

- difficulty concentrating
- feelings of worthlessness or excessive or inappropriate guilt
- hopelessness
- recurrent thoughts of death or suicide
- changes in appetite or sleep
- psychomotor agitation or retardation
- reduced energy or fatigue

The two lists are more or less the same. Both include physical and psychological items. Whereas the *DSM-5* lists weight loss or weight gain, the *ICD* speaks of appetite changes. Some people eat more in order to comfort themselves during depression and so gain weight. Others, probably the majority, lose their appetite and so lose weight. Both lists stipulate that the symptoms should have been experienced for a period of at least two weeks. In order to make the diagnosis; therefore, the doctor will ask questions about physical matters such as eating and sleeping, and about psychological aspects, such as the kind of thoughts that have been dominating the individual's thinking. Besides the signs and symptoms, doctors consider to what extent the person's ability to carry out their everyday tasks is affected. They will also want to know something of the person's family and social circumstances. Is there a history of depression in the family? Has there been a recent major stress in life? How much support does the person have from family and friends? An important question is whether the person is having suicidal thoughts. A decision will then be made as to how severe the depression is, and advice and treatment will be offered accordingly.[5]

Medical Treatment of Depression

Having listened to the patient, if the doctor suspects that the problem is mild depression, he or she may wish to monitor the person, and may recommend cognitive behavioral therapy, which helps people identify thought patterns and beliefs that might be contributing to the lowered mood.[6] In moderate to severe depression in which everyday functioning is impaired, antidepressant medication will be prescribed. Most people who are diagnosed with depression are able to be treated by the general practitioner. People with more severe illness will be referred to a psychiatrist, a medical doctor who is a specialist in the treatment of psychiatric mental disorder. In complex and particularly severe cases of depression that do not respond to treatment, the psychiatrist may prescribe electroconvulsive therapy, in which an electric shock is administered to the brain under general anesthetic. Sometimes it may be necessary for people suffering from depression to be admitted to psychiatric wards for treatment. This would be the case in particular if the patient showed considerable self-neglect, or if the patient was considered to be a danger to him- or herself.

THE COMPLEX NATURE OF DEPRESSION

Thus far, I have been describing the phenomenon of depression from a medical perspective. I have done this because in Western society the medical model has the most influence on people's lives. If we have a health condition and are unable to work, for example, we need a doctor to give permission to take time off. However, it must be said that the concept of

5. National Institute for Health and Care Excellence (NICE), "Depression in Adults."

6. Cognitive behavioral therapy (CBT) holds that depression is characterized by distorted or dysfunctional thinking. Sufferers of depression, who typically engage in negative thinking about themselves, the world, and their future, are helped to identify these automatic thoughts and core beliefs, learn how these relate to their mood, and replace them with healthy ones. Beck et al., *Cognitive Therapy of Depression*. See further Kennerley et al., *Introduction to Cognitive Behaviour Therapy*. Mindfulness-based cognitive therapy (MBCT) is recommended particularly for recurrent depression; it combines cognitive therapy with meditation and mindfulness techniques. See Segal et al., *Mindfulness-Based Cognitive Therapy for Depression*.

depression is far less simple than the lists given in the *DSM-5* and *ICD-11* might suggest. A major problem is that the idea that depression should be understood primarily as a disease seems to reduce its etiology to a matter of biology. While this may be the case with some kinds of depression, it is known that many people develop depression as a result of life circumstances such as loneliness or trauma. This has been recognized by the medical profession, which takes into account not only biological but psychological and social factors when diagnosing and treating depression.[7] However, some critics of psychiatry question the exclusivity of the medical model for treating depression. Dan Blazer, for example, argues that psychiatry has become dominated by the biomedical approach to such an extent that it has neglected the social and cultural forces which can contribute to the development of depression.[8] We will have reason to return to these questions later when we consider how our Christian communities can help care for people suffering from depression.[9] In the meantime, however, it is important for pastoral carers to acknowledge the complex nature of depression and that many factors might be influencing the experience of those whom we wish to help.

Checklists of the sort found in the *DSM-5* and *ICD-11*, which help doctors diagnose depression, are an important part of medical practice. They not only provide practitioners with guidance as to what to look for in a patient, but also represent the distillation of years of experience in observing and recording the behavior and appearance of people and in listening to what they have to say. Over the years there has been enough consistency in these observations and reports to be able to say that there is something which can be recognized as a "major depressive episode." However, these lists need to be used intelligently, sensitively, and wisely, and not regarded as the sole criteria for understanding depression. Practitioners are increasingly recognizing the need to have an understanding of an individual's circumstances, habits, and thought patterns, all of which may contribute to someone's low mood. Even when it can be established that there is a biomedical cause of the disease, it is known that a person's social

7. See Engel, "Clinical Application."

8. Blazer, *Age of Melancholy*.

9. It is recognized too that depression may be experienced and expressed in different ways in different cultures. See, for example, Chentsova-Dutton and Tsai, "Understanding Depression Across Cultural Contexts."; Eshun and Caldwell-Colbert, "Culture and Mood Disorders." Here I am concerned with depression as it is understood in Western societies, by which I mean primarily in Europe, North America, and Australia.

and psychological state can have a direct effect on his or her well-being at any given time.

Nevertheless, lists of symptoms and signs such as the diagnostic manuals provide give us a very impoverished view of the subjective *experience* of depression. For example, they tell us nothing of the physical pain that many sufferers report, the sheer terror of the condition, or why it can lead to suicide. Psychiatrists and psychologists are increasingly aware of this, and there is a growing emphasis on the importance of listening to and trying to understand what the individual is experiencing in the midst of depression.[10] As Rita Charon says in her book on narrative in medicine, "Only when the doctor understands to some extent what his or her patient goes through can medical care proceed with humility, trustworthiness, and respect."[11] As we shall see, similar changes have been taking place in our understanding of the nature of good pastoral care. It is not enough for us to know *that* the individual is suffering from clinical depression or to have some idea of how a medical doctor might attempt to help him or her; we also need to listen, in order to try to understand the kind of experience the depressed person is going through, how it is affecting life, and how it is impacting family and friends. If therefore we want to be able to help a person suffering from depression, it is crucial that we have some empathic understanding of the *experience* of depression, as well as some appreciation of the life circumstances of those who are suffering from it. Not only that, but from a pastoral perspective it is vital, as Tasia Scrutton emphasizes, that we appreciate something of how the depressed person interprets and understands the experience, for that will directly affect how we approach their pastoral care.[12]

ACCOUNTS OF DEPRESSION

Of course, we will never be able to understand completely what is going on in another person's mind. However, we can try to learn something of what it feels like to be depressed, and in this case, we are fortunate because many writers have described their experiences of the illness. These accounts range from the reports of ordinary people who are surveyed by medical

10. See, for example, Charon, *Narrative Medicine*; Crossley, *Introducing Narrative Psychology*; Sarbin, *Narrative Psychology*.

11. Charon, *Narrative Medicine*, 3–4.

12. Scrutton, *Christianity and Depression*.

sociologists, such as David Karp's *Speaking of Sadness*, to accounts of personal experience such as Andrew Solomon's *The Noonday Demon* or Lewis Wolpert's *Malignant Sadness*. These can give us far deeper insights into the experience of depression than clinical textbooks can provide.[13] Anthologies such as Nell Casey's *Unholy Ghost* provide accounts of the experiences of sufferers, but also perspectives from relatives, friends, and carers, on whom the impact of depression can be severe.[14]

The writers speak of their experience of the symptoms of depression, to which we have been referring—restless agitation, uncontrollable weeping, inability to sleep or sleeping too much, inability to concentrate, apathy, self-blame, and thoughts of death. They often resort to metaphor to describe this "pathological sadness" and its effects.[15] One of Karp's respondents speaks of his experience of depression as a feeling of drowning:

> I've referred to it as a dark storm at sea. The sea would, like, relate to the insecurity. You're going to sink. You're going to lose yourself, your life, your everything, and then sink to death. I guess, maybe the sea is death. And the dark storm is, I think, hopelessness. The sea is below you. There is a storm above you. It's a dark storm between your ears. That's how I see it . . . I mean it's doom, it's hopelessness, down the water is death, and up is just a dark storm, that you want to get away from but can't . . . That's why the sense of doom. And that causes a paralysis, you know . . . The sense of doom actually paralyzed you . . . It incapacitates you.[16]

Another of Karp's interviewees speaks of "a sense of being trapped, sort of like an animal, like a tiger pacing in a cage . . . I can't get out and it's night time and the daylight's never going to come."[17]

Writers often speak of the losses that depression brings: the loss of interest in things which would normally give pleasure (known as anhedonia), the loss of a sense of self-worth (sometimes even to the extent of self-loathing), the loss of the ability to sustain relationships or the ability to work, and even the loss of a sense of self altogether. They also speak of

13. Karp, *Speaking of Sadness*; Solomon, *The Noonday Demon*; Wolpert *Malignant Sadness*. See further Brampton *Shoot the Damn Dog*; Wurtzel, *Prozac Nation*; Galloway, *Trick Is to Keep Breathing*. See Oyebode, "Autobiographical Narrative and Psychiatry."

14. Casey, *Unholy Ghost*.

15. Wolpert, *Malignant Sadness*, 74.

16. Karp, *Speaking of Sadness*, 93.

17. Karp *Speaking of Sadness*, 94.

the loss of hope. Whereas mentally healthy people can look to the future and sense that there may be some form of rescue or escape from present suffering, that life will somehow improve, those who are depressed lose this ability. In his account William Styron describes the profound sadness, the deep emotional pain, the inability to take pleasure in anything, and the overriding sense of hopelessness which engulfed him at the worst stages of his illness:

> In depression this faith in deliverance, in ultimate restoration, is absent. The pain is unrelenting, and what makes the condition intolerable is the foreknowledge that no remedy will come—not in a day, an hour, a month, or a minute. If there is mild relief, one knows that it is only temporary; more pain will follow. It is the hopelessness even more than the pain that crushes the soul.[18]

Styron is saying that the depressive comes to believe that there is no hope ever of being without psychic pain. The pain feeds the sense of hopelessness that eventually crushes the soul—extinguishing even the will to live. Styron's language is striking—the depressive "knows" that no remedy will come, and that any relief is only temporary. There is no possibility of change for the better. What started as a sense of hopelessness that he will never get better becomes much more, developing into an all-pervasive sense that there is nothing to get better for. For Styron, the core of the hopelessness was that the illness, the pain, would not go away, that he would be condemned to live with it. And so he says that he began to think about suicide:

> Many of the artefacts of my house had become potential devices for my own destruction; the attic rafters (and an outside maple or two) a means to hang myself, the garage a place to inhale carbon monoxide, the bathtub a vessel to receive the flow from my open arteries.[19]

The sense of hopelessness of which Styron speaks is undoubtedly a source of great suffering, and constitutes a danger to life. The poet Jane Kenyon says something similar.

18. Styron, *Darkness Visible*, 61–62.

19. Styron, *Darkness Visible*, 52.

> CREDO
> Pharmaceutical wonders are at work
> But I believe only in this moment
> Of well-being. Unholy ghost,
> You are certain to come again.[20]

Kenyon speaks here of the fear of hoping that things will continue to be all right. Medication may be helping her in the short term, but she knows from experience that the depression will return. She may be able to cope at the moment, but the depression, which changes people's thoughts, will recur, and she will become someone else.

> Coarse, mean, you'll put your feet
> on the coffee table, lean back,
> and turn me into someone who can't
> take the trouble to speak; someone
> who can't sleep, or who does nothing
> but sleep; can't read, or call
> for an appointment for help.
> There is nothing I can do
> against your coming.[21]

The sense of powerlessness she feels over something that robs her of all enjoyment in life also robs her of hope. There is nothing to predict other than the fact that the depression will return. It is too much to hope for a better future with the constant threat and reality of depression hanging over her.

In such a state of severe emotional pain, the idea that there might be a future is barely comprehensible. It is hard enough to get through the day, let alone be able to imagine what good things might happen next week or next year. A sense of futility and pointlessness pervades. There is simply no point in looking ahead—all possibilities are lost.[22] In her memoir, Sally Brampton, who eventually did take her own life, wrote:

> Wanting to die goes hand in hand with the illness. It is a symptom of severe depression, not a character failing or moral flaw. Nor is it truly a desire to die so much as a fervent wish not to go on living. All depressives understand that distinction.[23]

20. Kenyon, *Collected Poems*, 231–35.

21. Kenyon, *Collected Poems*, 234.

22. Ratcliffe (*Experiences of Depression*, 66) speaks of the experience of depression as "loss of openness to the possibility of things changing in a good way."

23. Brampton, *Shoot the Damn Dog*, 2.

"Depression" she writes, "is a paralysis of hope."[24] Since those who are well are unlikely to understand this experience, many who suffer from severe depression of this sort can come to believe that it would be better if they were not around to spoil things for others, causing them to suffer too. So it is that thoughts of death become preoccupations, and suicide seems a reasonable option.

CHRISTIAN ACCOUNTS OF DEPRESSION

Christian accounts similarly describe the pain and anguish that depression brings. Gerard Manley Hopkins, the Jesuit poet, suffered from severe depression and wrote about it in what are now known as his "terrible sonnets." In his poem "No worst, there is none" he takes us into an inner mental world that is frightening, dark, wretched. He cries out for relief and receives none. He longs to escape his torture. What makes it worse is that he knows the torture comes from within; it cannot be blamed on anyone else. It may or may not have a cause, but it seems uncontrollable and, in fact, to be in control of him. The spiral of dark thoughts takes him further down: "more pangs will, schooled at forepangs, wilder wring."[25]

Hopkins gives voice to an experience with which many are familiar—a debilitating sense of darkness, an almost physical pain, and desperation. The eighteenth-century poet William Cowper, who suffered such serious depression that he attempted suicide on several occasions, wrote:

> The weather is an exact emblem of my mind in its present state. A thick fog envelops every thing, and at the same time it freezes intensely. You will tell me that this cold gloom will be succeeded by a cheerful spring, and endeavor to encourage me to hope for a spiritual change resembling it. But it will be lost labour: Nature revives again, but a soul once slain, lives no more. The hedge that has been apparently dead, is not so, it will burst into leaf and blossom at the appointed time; but no such time is appointed for the stake that stands in it. It is as dead as it seems, and will prove itself no dissembler.[26]

Cowper's words point to the sense of the loss of hope of which our secular writers have spoken. He describes the experience of being unable to rejoice

24. Brampton, *Shoot the Damn Dog*, 3.

25. Gerard Manley Hopkins, "No worst there is none" in Gardner, *Poems and Prose*, 61.

26. King and Ryskamp, *Letters and Prose Writings*, 200.

over the arrival of spring, but his own soul cannot revive with it, for it has been "slain." The hope that would normally come with spring is denied him.

Cowper writes about this spiritual suffering in his poem "The Castaway." He describes his depressed state as being "buried above ground." He recognizes that he is not the only one who has had this kind of experience, but what adds to his suffering is that God neither came to the rescue nor gave words of comfort.

> No voice divine the storm allayed,
> No light propitious shone,
> When, snatch'd from all effectual aid,
> We perished, each, alone;
> But I, beneath a rougher sea,
> And whelm'd in deeper gulphs than he.[27]

These words express the sheer terror which the loss of hope entails as well as the grief that is brought about by the realization that cherished beliefs about God are letting him down. The God in whom he has trusted is not rescuing him from this terrible suffering.

Modern-day writers express the same thoughts. Theologian Kathryn Greene-McCreight speaks of her depressive episodes as "hell, just unrelenting hell." She notes that hope for the Christian is the "drive toward the goal at the end of time, the divine healing of all creation." But, she says, in depression time stands still, and in the midst of a depressive episode she loses sight of the hope which is at the heart of her faith.[28] For the Baptist pastor John E Colwell, the sense of abandonment and "God-forsakenness" which he experiences in periods of depression brings to mind the words of Ps 22 that Jesus cried out on the cross: "Why have you forsaken me?"[29]

DEPRESSION AND HOPE

A sense of hopelessness is reported so often by sufferers of depression, both Christian and non-Christian, that it is surprising that it is not listed in the *DSM-5* checklist. While psychologists have long been aware of the part hopelessness plays in depression, they are undecided as to the exact

27. Baird and Ryskamp, *Poems of William Cowper*, 216. On Cowper see Sykes, "Wonders in the Deep."

28. Greene-McCreight, *Darkness Is My Only Companion*, 67. Other accounts include Cotter, *Brainsquall*; Hulme and Hulme, *Wrestling with Depression*.

29. Colwell, *Why Have You Forsaken Me?*

relationship between hope, hopelessness, and depression. An influential theory sees hopelessness as a cause of depression rather than a feature. According to this theory, people who have a negative pattern of thinking in which they cannot see positive outcomes to their experiences are more likely to be vulnerable to depression when negative life events take place.[30] There is also a continuing debate as to whether hope is a matter of cognition (i.e., thinking) or emotion. When we are hoping, are we thinking or feeling?[31] Perhaps the lack of clarity here complicates matters for therapists: What exactly are they attempting to treat when a patient speaks of hopelessness? Whatever the case, there is no doubt that the loss of existential hope is of real clinical concern not least because it can lead directly to loss of life through suicide.[32]

As far as pastoral care is concerned, it is encouraging that there is increasing recognition among clinicians that spirituality is an important aspect of mental illness which needs to be considered in assessment and treatment. Psychiatrist John R. Peteet, for example, has written on loss of hope as an additional burden for people of faith who experience depression.[33] This can bring a sense of abandonment and rejection, and tear at the very center of the Christian's sense of identity. Andrew Solomon writes,

> Depression is for many people an experience of being cast out by God or abandoned by Him, and many who have been depressed say they are unable to believe in a God who inflicts such cruelty so uselessly on the members of His flock.[34]

For Christians, the loss of hope can also exacerbate the sense of shame and isolation that is already inherent in the experience. What kind of Christian am I if I can see no future and no reason for living? It also brings isolation, for the simple reason that other believers may not understand what the person is going through, and may reject them on the grounds that their faith is somehow faulty or inferior. The experience of the loss of hope in depression is therefore a cause of pastoral concern, for the ability to hope

30. Seligman, *Helplessness.* Seligman's learned helplessness theory was later refined into the hopelessness theory of depression; Abramson et al., "Hopelessness Depression."

31. Hope is generally thought of as a cognitive construct. See the discussion in Cheavens and Ritschel, "Hope Theory." For more on the psychological views of hope, see Gallagher and Lopez, *Oxford Handbook of Hope.*

32. See Ratcliffe, *Experiences of Depression*, 99–127.

33. See Peteet, *Depression and the Soul.*

34. Solomon, *Noonday Demon*, 130.

is such a central part of Christian identity that its loss is a source of great spiritual suffering on top of already intolerable emotional distress. In such a situation it is surely the responsibility of pastoral carers to try to be agents of hope.

CONCLUSION

In this chapter we have explored the nature of depression, its medical treatment, and some experiential accounts by Christians and non-Christians. We have noted that a sense of hopelessness is a major aspect of many people's experiences of depression and that this is a matter of serious pastoral concern. Medical treatment of depression works on the assumption that in order to return to health, treatment will be given which will alleviate the symptoms and, where possible, tackle the cause of the depression. In other words, clinicians seek to remove the suffering, which in this case includes low mood and the sense of hopelessness associated with it. By alleviating suffering, they seek to restore hope to those who feel hopeless so that the person can return to a healthy, fruitful life.

What, then, are we to do with Rom 5:1–5, in which Paul says that for believers, suffering is something that should be boasted in, for it actually leads to hope? Paul's words seem to fly in the face of received medical wisdom. Can they have anything to say to the experience of depression at all? In order to answer this question we will now proceed to examine the text itself. We will undertake an initial exegesis of the passage with a view to understanding it in its historical and literary context. Then, adopting a foundationalist approach, we will ask how this text might inform the pastoral care of people suffering from depression.

3

Romans 5:1–5: A Foundationalist Approach

Therefore, since we are justified by faith, we have peace with God
through our Lord Jesus Christ, 2 through whom we have obtained
access to this grace in which we stand; and we boast in our hope
of sharing the glory of God. 3 And not only that, but we also boast
in our sufferings, knowing that suffering produces endurance, 4 and
endurance produces character, and character produces hope, 5 and
hope does not disappoint us, because God's love has been poured
into our hearts through the Holy Spirit that has been given to us.

—*Rom 5:1–5*

INTRODUCTION

We have seen that many people who suffer from depression speak of a loss of the ability to hope. This causes great suffering, and can ultimately be life-threatening. Given that hope is central to the life of faith, a sense of its loss is an additional burden for Christians, who can feel guilt and shame at a perceived spiritual failure and become isolated from their faith communities as a result. Clearly, there is a pastoral responsibility to help Christians who are feeling hopeless due to depression, and it is natural for us to turn to the Bible for help in the task. But what are we to make of Paul's words in Rom 5:1–5, in which he speaks of believers rejoicing and persevering in their suffering for this will bring about hope? Of what use can these words be in the pastoral care of people who have lost the ability to hope as a result of severe depression?

In this chapter, we will undertake an initial exegesis of Rom 5:1–5. Making use of historical criticism, we will ask what Paul might have wanted to say to the believers at Rome with regard to suffering and hope. In order to try to address this question our first task must be to set this passage in its literary context. Having done so, we will focus mainly, though not exclusively, on the rather dense train of thought in 5:3–4. What does it mean to say that rejoicing and persevering in suffering will lead to hope? Then, adopting a foundationalist approach, we will ask how this passage might help pastoral carers today to reach out to and offer help to people who are suffering from depression.

THE CONTEXT OF ROMANS 5:3–4

Paul's words on suffering and hope come in the context of a letter of introduction to the Roman church, which he intends to visit (15:23). He sends greetings (16:3–16), and asks for prayer as he takes a financial gift from churches in Macedonia and Achaia to believers in Jerusalem (15:23–33). Much of this long and complex letter, he explains in 15:15–16, is intended to introduce his ministry as apostle to the Gentiles. He is also probably defending this ministry against possible detractors, for the idea that the gospel is intended for both Jews and Gentiles has been giving rise to some problems, an example of which has arisen in the church at Rome. Confusion has arisen as to whether or not Gentile believers should be observing Jewish practices such as Sabbath and festivals and food laws (Rom 14:1—15:13) and the problem is serious enough to constitute a threat to unity. Paul is anxious that they should be able to learn to live and worship together, despite differences of opinion. Such differences should not be allowed to divert attention away from their primary raison d'etre—the worship of Christ (15:5–6).

In chapters 1–4, in order to introduce his thinking, Paul offers an extended discourse in which he explains what God has done through Jesus Christ.[1] He introduces the idea that those who are in a right relationship

1. For the various arguments as to why Paul wrote to the Roman churches, see

with God live lives characterized by the "obedience which comes from faith" (1:5).[2] However, the fact is that the whole of humanity, Jew and Gentile alike, has fallen into idolatry and sin. "All have sinned," he says in 3:23, "and fallen short of the glory of God." However, God has provided a way for all people (Jews and Gentiles alike) to find salvation *dia pisteōs Iēsou Christou* (3:22), a phrase that is usually translated as "faith in Jesus Christ" (3:22). We will explore what this might mean in some depth later, but for now the important thing to note is that Paul is insisting that salvation comes though faith rather than through any human effort.[3] Just as God considered Abraham to be righteous because of his faith (4:22) and not because of any effort of his own, so now believers in Jesus, regardless of ethnicity, have been "justified" and given access to God's grace through the work of Jesus Christ.

These initial chapters, then, tell the story of God's dealings with all humanity, the story of "incongruous grace" and redemption through the work of Jesus Christ to people who do not deserve it.[4] As Beverley Roberts Gaventa emphasizes, the stress is on the fact that God has acted for *all* people, Jew and Gentile alike, and this understanding will be crucial background for Paul's pastoral intervention in the problems that are threatening the unity of the Roman church.[5] Having thus set the scene, in 5:1 Paul now turns his attention to some of the implications of his Roman recipients' being "justified by faith." Because of Jesus' death and resurrection, believers have been reconciled with God.[6] This means that they now find themselves in a wholly new way of being: they have peace with God and stand in a state of grace—the undeserving recipients of divine generosity (5:2). They also have hope—hope that they should be proud of—for one day, they will share

---

Donfried, *Romans Debate*. Also Das, *Solving the Romans Debate*, 9–52.

2. This is the majority understanding of the phrase "obedience of faith." See Moo, *Romans*, 52.

3. In the course of his argument Paul also discusses the place of Jewish law in the life of the church. This has been the subject of intense debate, which we need not enter into here. For "new perspective" scholars, Paul is taking issue with people who take pride in Jewish identity, whether this is expressed in the adherence to identity markers such as circumcision or in (misplaced) nationalism. The more traditional "Lutheran" view is that Paul is concerned with the belief that salvation could be earned by adherence to Jewish law. For an overview of the discussion, see Horrell, *Introduction to the Study of Paul*, 125–52.

4. Barclay, *Paul and the Gift*.

5. Gaventa, *When in Romans*, 30ff.

6. Here, along with most commentators, I understand *echōmen* and *kauchōmetha* to be indicative. See Dunn, *Romans 1–8*, 245. However, see also Jewett, *Romans*, 348; and Gaventa, *Romans*, 139, who favor the subjunctive.

in the glory of God (5:3). In the chapters that follow, Paul will go on to say that because of this grace they are free from the power of sin and death. He will tell them that they now have a new life of the Spirit (6:10–11), having become children and heirs in the family of God (8:14–17). And one day, they will share in the divine glory (8:17) when it is fully revealed. The church, as Michael J. Gorman says, is a place in which "life and peace are springing forth."[7]

But this raises a question. Assurance of future hope is one thing (and certainly something to rejoice in), but what about the here and now? The stark reality of suffering cannot be brushed aside. Perhaps anticipating a possible objection, Paul says in verses 3–4, believers "boast" or rejoice when trouble comes because perseverance in suffering leads to a tested character, which leads to hope. In order to think about this extraordinary statement, and what its significance might be for us today, we need to unpack the sequence of thought, considering each component in turn.

UNPACKING ROMANS 5:3–4

The first word in the sequence is *thlipsis*, which is often translated as "suffering" but can also mean "trial," "trouble," or "tribulation." When Paul wrote this letter to the church in Rome, he may have had persecution in mind, as the church struggled to live in a hostile environment in the Roman Empire. The term, however, can refer to trials and hardships of all kinds, and need not be limited to persecution.[8] Paul may have been thinking about the struggles of a young church, made up of people from various backgrounds and traditions who were learning to live together in community; to these struggles and difficulties Paul will return later in the letter. Or he could be using *thlipsis* to refer to a more generalized suffering that is part and parcel of living in the "now and not yet." In any case, suffering and trials, Paul says, bring about *hupomonē*, which the NRSV translates as "endurance." Other equally valid translations are "perseverance," "patience," and "fortitude." The term denotes a "moral strength" in which we do not allow trouble to defeat us. If we are able to withstand trials without collapsing under the strain, we are persevering. And if we persevere rather than give up at the first whiff of suffering, we will become stronger.

7. Gorman, *Romans*, 148–49.

8. See the discussion of the term *thlipsis* in Still, *Conflict in Thessalonica*, 208ff.

The next term in the sequence is *dokimē*, which probably should be understood as "tested character."[9] The term is problematic, for it has no referent. Traditionally, it is understood to refer to believers, in which case it will mean that perseverance brings about a tried and tested character. John Ziesler, however, thinks it refers to "God's constant support," which is "tested and found adequate." He thus translates, "endurance proves God's sustaining power."[10] Nevertheless, since the suffering of which Paul has been speaking is best understood as affecting human beings, it seems likely that *dokimē* has to do with people too. The idea is akin to that of "character building." Persevering in suffering produces people who are strong, resilient and productive. Character is revealed by patterns of behavior, how we respond to adversity and trials, how we relate to others, and our ethical concerns. We speak of people who consistently make good moral decisions, who have integrity, as having "strong character." They are the people whom others respect, who set a good example, and whose lives are attractive and coherent. "Weak" characters are those who crumble under the strain, who seize up. Clearly, without perseverance, the "tested" character to which Paul refers here will not become evident.

The Meaning of Hope in This Passage

In his view that *thlipsis* leads to character, Paul is in step with contemporary Greco-Roman and Jewish writers, who believed that suffering was to be valued as disciplinary, educative, and refining.[11] However, he goes much further. It is at the end of this process, according to verse 5, that hope (*elpis*) comes about. Those who develop strength of character are able to have hope. The question is, what does Paul mean by hope? On one level, we can understand the whole sequence of thought (suffering—perseverance—character—hope) as a statement of common sense. The more we persevere in suffering, the stronger our characters become, and the more we can cope with adversity. Learning from experience, we develop the ability to see that mistakes, setbacks, and misfortune need not be crippling, and that things can improve. A simple analogy for this is a child learning to walk. As the

9. Moo, *Romans*, 303; although see Jewett, *Romans* 354–55, who thinks it refers to a tested faith.

10. Ziesler, *Paul's Letter to the Romans*, 138–39.

11. Talbert, *Learning Through Suffering*.

child learns that when it falls, if it gets up, it will be able to get its balance and walk even further—so it becomes more resilient.[12]

In this sense, hope becomes a state of mind, or expectation, in which we think there is good reason that our desires might be fulfilled. As Paul O'Callaghan notes, hope adds to such desires "the inner conviction that *it is possible* to obtain or possess the object desired, in spite of the difficulty in doing so. In other words, the desired goal is *an arduous yet possible one*."[13] In short, hope is a positive attitude of mind that enables us to carry on from day to day. When we think in this way we are telling ourselves that there are good reasons for working toward the future—whether in a general feeling that difficulties can be overcome, or in a desire for something in particular to happen. Whatever it might be, this hope has a "sustaining power."[14]

So, perseverance in suffering leads to stronger character both in a moral and a spiritual sense. We become more able to understand not only our personal ways of coping with adversity, but also the way God works in the world and in our lives. In the Biblical literature, the idea that withstanding trials, with the attendant strengthening of character, leads to a deepening in faith in the sense of trusting in God, is not unique to Paul. In Sir 2:4–6, for example we read,

> Accept whatever befalls you,
> and in times of humiliation be patient.
> For gold is tested in the fire,
> and those found acceptable, in the furnace of humiliation.
> Trust in him, and he will help you;
> make your ways straight, and hope in him.

In the New Testament, the Epistle of James speaks in terms similar to Paul's (Jas 1:2–4), and 1 Pet 1:6–7 reads,

> In this you rejoice, even if now for a little while you have had to suffer various trials, so that the genuineness of your faith—being more precious than gold that, though perishable, is tested by fire—may be found to result in praise and glory and honor when Jesus Christ is revealed.

These writers are agreed that suffering strengthens character and that the process brings about hope. Paul, however, is distinctive in his reassurance

12. See Keshgegian, *Time for Hope*, 188.

13. O'Callaghan, *Christ Our Hope*, 4 (italics original).

14. Martin, *How We Hope*, 7.

that we are not left alone as we try to persevere. Our deepening understanding is made possible by the work of the Holy Spirit, who pours God's love into our hearts (Rom 5:5). Hope, therefore, is an attitude of mind which is based on the knowledge of God's love for us, not only because of what he has done through Christ in the past, but because of our experience of his continuing work through the Holy Spirit. It is this which spurs us on from day to day; it is this that makes life worth living.

However, it is also clear that this hope has a specific content. In 5:2, Paul speaks of a hope that we will one day "share in the glory of God." What this means has already been hinted at in chapter 3. There, at verse 23, Paul states that everyone has sinned and fallen short of the glory of God: human beings do not match up to the splendor that characterizes God. They should—but they do not, because they have opted to go their own way (Rom 1:21–23). In their arrogance they have exchanged this glory for something far inferior. This should, strictly speaking, put them in a hopeless position—they will never be what God intended them to be. However, the message of the gospel is that through Christ's work the hope of one day sharing the glory of God has been restored.[15] In other words, hope is eschatological in orientation. The content of Christian hope is "what Christ does to our future."[16]

What this means becomes clearer in Rom 8:18–25. Believers' present sufferings come about because of the struggle with sin in the world.[17] But this should be seen in the perspective of the glory that will one day be revealed to them (8:18). What they see now is only partial; one day the full glory of God, 'the radiant splendor of the presence of God," will be revealed to all.[18] Further, in 8:18 the Greek phrase is *eis hēmas*. In the NRSV this is

15. As Edward Adams points out, there are two strands of thought regarding the future of the cosmos in the New Testament—one (as here) that anticipates a nondestructive transformation, and another, represented in e.g., 2 Pet 3:5–13 and Heb 12:25–9, that envisages an apocalyptic catastrophe, resulting in a dissolution of the created universe. That these two strands can coexist in the canon should warn us against trying to predict exactly what will happen at the end-times. Whatever happens, the triumph of God will be seen, and it is this which provides the narrative of hope for believers. See Adams, *Stars Will Fall*, 257. See further Hill, *In God's Time*. For an overview of the concept of eschatological hope throughout Christian history see Hebblethwaite, *Christian Hope*.

16. Brunner, *Faith, Hope, and Love*, 48.

17. Jervis, *At the Heart of the Gospel*, 77–127.

18. Cobb and Lull, *Romans*, 123. See also Jewett, *Romans*, 510: "The originally intended glory of the creation shall yet be restored, including specifically the glory we humans were intended to bear."

translated as "the glory of God will be revealed to us." But, as in the KJV and NIV, it can also be translated as "in us." All the might, honor, and splendor that belong to God, and which human beings were originally intended to reflect (Ps 8:1, 5–6), will one day be revealed in believers too. They look forward to a time when they will be revealed as the children of God (18:17b), when they come to share in the revelation of the glory of God, and the whole of creation will be released from its bondage to decay and returned to its original splendor.[19] To put it another way, believers will be "conformed to the image of [God's] Son" (8:29), becoming just like Christ himself in all his perfection. Hope, as John Webster puts it, is the "confident longing for full realization of life in Christ."[20]

This future hope gives their suffering eternal significance. The sufferings of the present time, says Paul, are nothing compared to the glory that they will one day see, and in which they will share. However, this does not mean that what they go through now is futile. Rather, it is a necessary part of their identification with Christ as his co-heirs—for they are sharing in his sufferings and so participating in his continuing work in the "now and not yet."[21] Believers thus see their lives and sufferings, as N. T. Wright says, as part of a "larger reality."[22]

The Relationship Between Suffering and Hope in the Life of the Believer

This initial analysis of Rom 5:1–5 suggests that Paul is describing what happens in the life of believers when they encounter suffering. In one sense, perseverance in trial and trouble leads to resilience as they learn from experience that the future can hold good things for them if they do not allow circumstances to crush them. The strength of character that builds up as they persevere brings about not merely a strengthening in their psyches but a greater understanding of the way God works in their lives. In this way, all suffering can bring about hope for the believer—and that is why they rejoice in it. If they persevere in their pain, they will become stronger

19. For a discussion of how this might (or might not) relate to the environmental issues such as climate change, see Horrell, *Bible and the Environment*.

20. Webster, "Hope," 302.

21. See Jervis, *At the Heart of the Gospel*, 125.

22. Wright, *Surprised by Hope*, 174. For a fuller discussion of the significance of suffering in Romans see Wu, *Suffering in Romans*.

in character and this, in turn, will enable them to hold on to the hope that things will be better at the end-times.

Moreover, believers in Christ are not overwhelmed by their sufferings, because they see them in eschatological perspective. Human existence has a *telos*—a goal and end point. The resurrection, the first glimpse of the future hope, has taken place, and they can live in this "now and not yet" period, confident that one day God will be all in all (see 1 Cor 15:28). Their lives are rooted in their faith in God and in the knowledge that he has acted in history though Jesus Christ, with the added assurance provided by the Holy Spirit, who pours the God's love into their hearts (Rom 5:5). Douglas Moo writes, "It is this internal, subjective—yes, even emotional—sensation within the believer that God does indeed love us—love expressed and made vital in real, concrete actions on our behalf—that gives to us the assurance that 'hope will not disappoint us.'"[23]

Not only do Christian believers have something to look forward to, but this promise for the future puts present sufferings into an entirely different perspective—they are temporary (so believers are enabled to persevere and become stronger) and have eternal significance. This hope arises from the knowledge of what God has done in Christ and what he will do in the future, and is sustained by the experience of the work of the Holy Spirit in our lives in the present.

PASTORAL APPLICATION FROM A FOUNDATIONALIST PERSPECTIVE

Paul's words here were intended to encourage a diverse community of new believers who were struggling to cope with life in first-century Rome. He wanted them to see that suffering (whatever form it might take) was not a cause for discouragement but rather for rejoicing. For, by persevering in times of trouble believers would develop the spiritual and moral strength that would enable them to appreciate the future hope which was theirs. We must now consider how these words might inform the pastoral care of those suffering from severe depression in our contemporary church communities. We will do this from a foundationalist perspective, which, as we have seen, tends to see Scripture as a book of propositions and instruction and so approaches the text with the question, "What ought I to do?" in

23. Moo, *Romans*, 305.

mind. How does this passage help us to maintain hope and be agents of hope to others in times of suffering?

According to Douglas Moo, Paul's intention here is to encourage "any who are faltering or downhearted to contemplate again what he or she has in Christ."[24] No matter what we are going through, we need to remind ourselves of the truths in this passage, and the contemplation of them will prevent us from despairing and giving up. In a slightly different vein, L. Ann Jervis writes, "We may experience and interpret and respond to our inevitable sufferings by claiming our place 'in Christ.' From the vantage of this 'in Christ' place, sufferings may be regarded as bounded by life and love and hope. It is possible from this perspective even to know peace and joy at the same times as we suffer."[25]

Similarly, in his commentary on Romans, Paul J. Achtemeier says of Rom 5:1–5:

> To whom do we turn in times of perplexity, in times when personal examination leads us to the edge of despair? Our text, particularly verses 1–5 with their message of peace, grace, hope, and confidence, helps us to move through the problem and to find the answer in a hope born of the assurance of the divine love shown in Christ. The deliverance from death Christ received in his resurrection is the assurance of our certain deliverance by the same God, who will defeat our sin and death as well.[26]

In each case, the author is suggesting that Paul's message here is this: when suffering comes, what we need to do is to remember what God has done in the past, acknowledge what he is continuing to do, and look forward to what will take place in the future.[27] If we do this, we will be able to get through. In other words, the key to being able to hold on to hope in the midst of suffering is to remember what we have been taught, and live accordingly. The foundationalist influence is evident in all of these writers. As they read the text, they are looking to see how believers should respond to suffering. In other words, they are asking, "When I, a believer, encounter suffering, what ought I to do?" This question leads them (perhaps unconsciously) to

24. Moo, *Romans*, 314.

25. Jervis, *At the Heart of the Gospel*, 122.

26. Achtemeier, *Romans*, 92–93.

27. Everts "Hope," 416: "Hope is the source of present strength for believers because it is grounded in what God has done in Christ, is experienced in the power of the Spirit and moves toward the glory that is to be revealed."

assume that the indicatives of the passage contain an implied imperative.[28] That is, they tend to assume that Paul's description of the way things are as a result of Christ's coming contains an implied instruction as to how we should respond in our everyday lives.

From this perspective, it seems that the onus is on the person experiencing suffering to persevere, to continue to trust and hold on to the hope that trust engenders. When it comes to using these verses in the pastoral care of someone who is going through difficult times, it is natural, also, that pastoral carers should see it as their responsibility to pass the instruction on. Those who are suffering should be encouraged to hold on to what they know of their relationship with God as a result of the work of Christ and of the future hope that is theirs as believers.

Now, there is no doubt that this kind of exhortation can be of help to many in certain circumstances. It is easy for us, in the midst of crisis, to lose sight of the tenets of our faith, and to allow fear and distress to commandeer our thinking. At such times, a reminder of the hope we have in Christ can be deeply reassuring and comforting. Without denigrating this view, however, and with great respect for those for whom these verses do provide comfort in this way, I suggest that there are certain difficulties with this approach with regard to the pastoral care of people suffering from depression. First, it assumes that in times of suffering Christians *are* able to hold on to what they have been taught and to find encouragement from it. Of course, for many people, this may be true. However, the person suffering from depression may find it next to impossible to do so. As we have seen from the accounts in the previous chapter, in periods of profound mental distress the deep certainties of faith that have sustained us throughout our lives may be called into question. Even if those who suffer from depression are able to continue to believe that Christ died for them, the chances are that if doubt sets in at all, they will be consumed with self-blame for not being the good Christian they think they ought to be.

Second, it is true that many people derive great comfort from the experience of God's love in their lives. However, in depression, emotional understanding of God's love is very often evasive. The "sensation" of God's

28. The idea of the indicative and imperative in Paul is usually discussed in relation to ethics. See Furnish, *Theology and Ethics in Paul*, and the critique offered in Rabens, "Indicative and Imperative." Here, I am suggesting that a foundationalist hermeneutic which looks for propositional certainty can lead readers to see implied indicatives and imperatives in passages that are not directly concerned with ethics, but with Christian living in general.

love, as Moo calls it,[29] is often lacking. Indeed, in a severe depression, it is common for sufferers to be prone to thinking that God does not, cannot love such a vile individual as he or she is. As we have already noted, depression can bring about a crisis of faith in which sufferers lose the idea that God loves them altogether. They are unable to feel the reality of spiritual comfort, and may feel very guilty as a result.

Third, the ability to look forward to a better time is well-nigh impossible. People suffering from severe depression often speak of being unable to see beyond today, let alone to hold on to the hope of one day being revealed as a son or daughter of God at the end-times. This may be because of the change in thinking which depression brings about, or because experience now challenges what was once taken as an unassailable truth. Whatever the reason, there is a need for tangible reassurance *now*—not just a promise of something that is to take place at the end-times. It is hard enough to battle through from day to day, without having to hang on for an eschatological promise that can, in Ernest Bloch's words, seem to be "empty promises of another world."[30]

Besides these difficulties in applying Rom 5:1–5 to the experience of depression, there is a further problem. If we see an implied imperative in this passage, it is natural to infer that Christians *should* be able to persevere in suffering and hold on to hope. They *should* be able to remember what Christ has done and live accordingly. Unfortunately, however, this way of reading the passage also carries the implication that those who are unable to do so must be at fault, and that their faith must be called into question. From this perspective, it is hard to avoid the conclusion that the person who has lost the ability to hope is somehow less than a good Christian, not up to the mark, and that it is the pastoral carer's duty to correct the fault. As we have seen, however, in the case of severe depression, this could compound the suffering of the individual, increasing the shame and guilt which they already feel—in other words, adding spiritual problems to an already deeply painful situation.

CONCLUSION

In this chapter an initial exegesis of Rom 5:1–5 has been carried out, focusing on the link between suffering and hope in verses 3–4. It has been

29. Moo, *Romans*, 305.

30. Bloch, *Principle of Hope*, 1198.

suggested that Paul sees persevering in suffering and holding on to a future hope as the natural response to knowing what God has done through Jesus Christ. On the basis of what they know about God's work in the past (faith), in the present (love), and in the future (hope), Christians are able persevere in suffering, and even rejoice, for they know that they will grow in spiritual and moral maturity as they await the full revelation of God's glory at the end-times. We then asked how these words might inform the pastoral care of people suffering from severe depression. Adopting a foundationalist perspective, which looks to the text for instruction for individual believers, we concluded that these words could be used to encourage, comfort, and exhort people who find themselves in difficult circumstances to remember what they know and have experienced, to persevere in their sufferings, and to press on into the future.

While I acknowledge that such a reading of the text is and has been of great comfort and strength to many throughout the centuries, I would like to suggest that it is of limited use in the pastoral care of depression. This is because, as we have seen, those who suffer from depression often find that holding on to cherished beliefs and envisaging a future hope is very difficult, if not impossible. Moreover, a well-meaning pastoral carer who adopts a foundationalist hermeneutic could infer that all that is required is to remind those who are suffering of what they (should) already know and to exhort them to obey the instruction. However, such an approach could well be counterproductive. Those suffering from depression may well be unable to respond to such counsel and may interpret it as condemnatory. They may even conclude that they are somehow failing as Christians.

Rather than dispense with this text altogether, I would like to suggest an alternative reading which may help us to avoid these pitfalls and offer a more fruitful way of helping pastoral carers to be agents of hope to those who feel hopeless as a result of depression. Please note that I am not dismissing the foundationalist approach out of hand, but merely suggesting that it might be of limited use, and that our understanding of how Paul's words might inform pastoral care could be enriched and deepened by looking at the text in a different way—namely, through the lens of character ethics. Before we do this, however, some groundwork needs to be done, and in the next chapter I will introduce character ethics and discuss its suitability as a hermeneutical lens for interpreting Paul's thought.

4

Character Ethics as a Hermeneutical Lens

"Saints cannot exist without a community, as they require, like all of us, nurturance by a people who, while often unfaithful, preserve the habits necessary to learn the story of God."

—*Stanley Hauerwas*

INTRODUCTION

In the last chapter, we conducted an initial exegesis of Rom 5:1–5. Adopting a foundationalist perspective, we then considered how these words might be used in the pastoral care of people with severe depression, approaching the text with the question, "What ought I to do?" in mind. It was suggested that, in the pastoral setting, Paul's words could be used to encourage, comfort, and exhort those who find themselves in difficulty, reminding them of what they know, and urging them to persevere and to keep their future hope before them. However, we saw too that while many people may find this approach helpful, the use of this text in this way may not be beneficial for those suffering from severe depression, and may even be counterproductive. But does this mean that Paul's words here are of no use at all in the pastoral care of depression? I believe that it does not, and that adopting a different hermeneutic can yield a richer interpretation that, in turn, will provide a much more fruitful understanding of how Paul's words might inform pastoral care of those who feel hopeless.

Those who read Scripture from a foundationalist hermeneutic tend to be seeking knowledge, instruction, and "absolute, incontestable certainty" from the text.[1] There is little doubt that over the years many people have found this way of reading Scripture to be helpful and comforting. However, as Stanley Hauerwas says, this starting point has certain consequences. The need for knowledge and instruction tends to lead readers of Scripture to see it as a book of propositions and rules that are given so that readers may live in the "right" way.[2] That is to say, Scripture is reduced to a repository of instructions and the Christian life to a matter of obedience and "correct" behavior. Fortunately, recent developments in ethical theory suggest an alternative hermeneutical lens that may help us to avoid such a reductionist view.

Character ethics moves us away from commands and rules as the sole basis for moral behavior. Although it recognizes a place for these, character ethics suggests that rather than ask what we ought to be doing in any given situation, we should ask a prior and more basic question: What kind of people ought we to be? If we are developing good character, it is argued, good moral behavior will naturally ensue, and we will build up healthy communities. The idea of the virtues is important here, and so are those of community, narrative, and wisdom. These concepts, I believe, open up a way of interpreting Rom 5:1–5 that can provide a more fruitful and compassionate approach to its use in the pastoral care of people suffering from severe depression, and they will be essential for our exploration of the passage in chapters to follow.

Before we can undertake this task, however, we must gain some understanding of character ethics and ask whether it is appropriate as a hermeneutical lens for reading Paul's letter. We will begin by exploring the idea of the virtues, which are not only central to contemporary character ethics but have played an important role in the history of Christian theology over the centuries.

1. Grenz and Franke, *Beyond Foundationalism*, 23.

2. Hauerwas, *Community of Character*, 53–71.

THE VIRTUES

The idea of the virtues goes back as far as Plato, but it is Aristotle's discussion in *Nicomachean Ethics* which has been most influential.[3] Aristotle said that in order to live happy lives and to flourish as human beings, it is necessary for us to develop certain habits. It is good, for example, to be courageous: if we act with courage, lives can be saved and much can be accomplished in difficult situations. The person who exercises the virtue of courage will contribute to the good in society and to his or her overall happiness. However, it is important to understand that the virtue of courage is the mean between two extremes: if we have too little courage, we will not achieve anything, and if we have too much, we may take too many risks and expose ourselves and others to danger.[4]

Virtues such as fortitude, temperance, prudence, and justice (known as the four cardinal virtues) are acquired through habit and practice. They are attitudes of mind which can be developed—learned, according to Aristotle, through doing.[5] We need consciously to choose to behave in virtuous ways in order to live well and achieve *eudaimonia*, which may be defined as "a fulfilled and fulfilling life." As we develop these attitudes of mind and act on them, they become embedded deep within our being, bringing about a state that can be "sustained even in the most difficult moments of our lives, and that endures over time."[6] Other virtues include friendship, generosity, truthfulness, gentleness, fairness, and self-control. Qualities such as these are necessary for us to be able to live alongside other people, and to build up flourishing and stable communities. Without them we would live selfishly, pleasing only ourselves.[7] People who exercise the virtues are considered to be people of good character: they not only have their own interests in view, but also recognize the importance of behaving in a certain way so that society as a whole can flourish.

3. Overviews of the philosophical literature on virtue are provided in Crisp and Slote, *Virtue Ethics*, 1–26; Hursthouse, *On Virtue Ethics*, 1–25.

4. "Every virtue is a summit between two vices, a crest between two chasms: hence courage stands between cowardice and temerity, dignity between servility and selfishness, gentleness between anger and apathy, and so on" (Comte-Sponville, *Short Treatise on the Great Virtues*, 5).

5. Aristotle, *Nichomachean Ethics* II, 1, 1103a33 in Aristotle, *Basic Works of Aristotle*, 952.

6. Cunningham, *Christian Ethics*, 151.

7. Russell, "Introduction," 1.

Christian theologians considered faith, hope, and love to be distinctive theological virtues, complementing the cardinal virtues listed above. For Thomas Aquinas (c. 1225–1274), "Virtue is a good quality of the mind, by which we live righteously, of which no one can make bad use, which God brings about in us, without us."[8] Just as prudence, justice, temperance, and patience are some of the "distinctive excellences" necessary for a good life, so faith, hope, and love are the "distinctive excellences" necessary for the development of *Christian* character and communities.[9] Importantly, for Aquinas, the aim (*telos*) of exercising the virtues is not to live happy lives, as it was for Aristotle, but to live righteously, and have union with God.[10]

Aquinas taught that the virtues come from two sources. They can be acquired through observing, learning, and imitating, or they can be God-given ("infused"). The moral virtues are acquired. The four cardinal virtues (fortitude, temperance, prudence, and justice) can be both acquired and "infused." The theological virtues (faith, hope, and love) are given ("infused") by God in order to enable the Christian community to fulfil its purpose, which is to worship and serve God. Faith, for example, relates to God as a source of knowledge, while hope relates to God as a source of goodness.[11]

Following the Reformation, the idea of the virtues fell into disuse in ethical discussion as deontology and utilitarianism gained ground. However, in 1958 the philosopher Elizabeth Anscombe published work in which she argued that both Kantian ethics and consequentialism were inadequate in their accounts of ethical living, and that we should bring the idea of virtue back into discussions of ethics. Thereafter, philosophers began to take up the idea and in the 1980s Alasdair MacIntyre's profoundly influential book *After Virtue* reintroduced Aristotle's ideas to a wide reading public.[12]

In *After Virtue* MacIntyre argues that a focus on character and virtue is a necessary corrective to the individualism and bureaucracy which became so characteristic of twentieth-century Western life. We are somehow dehumanized by the reduction of morality to obeying rules. Personal

8. Thomas Aquinas, *Summa Theologica*, I-II.55.4.

9. For overviews of the theological literature on the virtues, see especially Porter, "Recent Studies in Aquinas's Virtue Ethic"; Hibbs, "Interpretations of Aquinas's Ethics."

10. Thomas Aquinas, *Summa Theologica*, I-II.63.3.

11. Thomas Aquinas, *Summa Theologica*, II-II.17.6.

12. MacIntyre, *After Virtue*; Anscombe, *Ethics, Religion, and Politics*, 26–42; Foote, *Virtues and Vices and Other Essays*; Murdoch, *Sovereignty of Good*.

morality, MacIntyre insists, must take into account the well-being of society as a whole. Shared narratives give us a sense of community identity and convey to us the values by which we are to live. It is through the telling of stories that children learn the values of the society in which they are being brought up. For example, many fairy stories teach virtues such as integrity and goodness. According to this way of thinking, then, rather than focusing on obedience to rules, a healthy society will cultivate the virtues, which are essential for good character. So it is that people will learn to live wisely, making good decisions, which lead in turn to flourishing and healthy societies.

In character ethics, then, emphasis moves away from ideas of duty and act (that is, what we ought to be doing) to character (that is, what kind of people we ought to be). Character development through the practice of the virtues is central, and there is a shift of focus from the rights and wrongs of individual behavior to a valuing of the community of like-minded people who are working within shared stories and traditions, practices and aims. Thus, according to virtue ethics, will our communities flourish.

HAUERWAS'S CHARACTER ETHICS

The idea of the virtues has always been of interest to Roman Catholic moral theologians.[13] Protestants have been slower to be convinced, as we shall see below.[14] However, the work of the theologian Stanley Hauerwas has become deeply influential in bringing the idea of the virtues back into Protestant theological discourse.[15] Hauerwas maintains that Christian ethics (especially Protestant Christian ethics) has tended to revolve around the ideas of command and obedience. While not suggesting that these should be discounted altogether, he sees that we have much to learn from the traditional (Catholic) emphasis on character and virtue. Hauerwas is concerned that Christians have fallen into the trap of individualism, and have become preoccupied with their own personal morality and salvation. He argues that the sense of community that should characterize the church is in danger of being lost, and indeed that it may even have been lost already. However,

13. See, for example, Cessario, *Moral Virtues and Theological Ethics.*

14. Some are actively opposed. See, for example, O'Donovan, *Resurrection and Moral Order.* O'Donovan rejects much of virtue ethics on the grounds that it is relativistic.

15. See in particular Hauerwas, *Community of Character.* On the place of virtue ethics in Christian ethics see also Cunningham, *Christian Ethics*, 145–65.

Christians cannot live in isolation: our belief is grounded in a story in which everyone has a part to play. The story that gives us our identity is the story of God's intervention in history through Jesus Christ, and as we read it, we learn of the values that are to inform our lives and characterize our communities. We learn from the stories of the patriarchs and prophets, but above all we find them in the stories of Jesus' life, death, and resurrection, and we practice them because we want to conform to his example.[16]

Hauerwas understands character in terms of moral strength, which entails qualities (virtues) such as integrity, incorruptibility, and consistency. Character is the "orientation we give to our lives by ordering our desires, affections, and actions according to certain reasons rather than others."[17]

For a Christian, this orientation is provided by the "conviction that Christ through his life and death has decisively established God's kingdom."[18] Christians look to Christ to show them what kind of character they should have; it is from him that perfection is learned.[19] Christian communities are made up of people who are living in the continuing story or narrative brought about by the death and resurrection of Christ, and who know they have a part to play in it. In other words, they are "communities of character" with shared tradition and practices, in which human beings can be transformed into disciples of Christ.[20]

Hauerwas's ideas have become profoundly influential in Christian theology and ethics, and we shall be indebted to them in our use of character ethics as a hermeneutical lens for our passage in Romans.[21] Before we proceed, however, we need to note two important objections to the idea of the virtues and character as a basis for Christian ethics. Gilbert Meilaender protests that the idea of the virtues carries within it an unhealthy desire for perfectionism, which ultimately is egotistical in nature and so incompatible with *agapē* love. He also worries that it undercuts the idea of grace. In other words, when we focus on practicing the virtues, we become too concerned

16. Hauerwas, *Community of Character*, 96.

17. Hauerwas, *Character and the Christian Life*, 203.

18. Hauerwas, *Peaceable Kingdom*, 34.

19. Hauerwas, *Peaceable Kingdom*, 76.

20. On the importance of the link between character, community, and story see Bondi, "Elements of Character."

21. Following Hauerwas, we will from now on refer to character ethics rather than virtue ethics. On the nuances of the two terms, see Cahill, "Christian Character," 6.

with our own efforts and less cognizant of God's generous sovereignty in our lives. Meilaender notes,

> A sketch of the virtues is a picture of a fulfilled life, of the successful realization of a self. Such an approach cannot without difficulty be incorporated into a vision of the world which has as its center a crucified God—which takes, that is, not self-realization but self-sacrifice as its central theme. Furthermore, the very notion of character seems to suggest . . . habitual behavior, abilities within our power, an acquired possession. And this in turn may be difficult to reconcile with the Christian emphasis on grace, the sense of the sinner's constant need of forgiveness, and the belief that we can have no claims upon the freedom of God.[22]

It is, however, possible to conceive of the virtues in a way that helps mitigate against these criticisms. First, we may counter the notion that practicing the virtues has to do with gaining perfection or self-actualization by noting the emphasis within character ethics on the idea of community. We practice patience and courage (for example) with a view to contributing to the well-being and flourishing of the community as a whole. Self-improvement, in other words, growth in character, may well be a by-product of exercising these virtues, but it is not the primary reason for doing so. In Hauerwas's terms, practicing the virtues is the way to bring about the peace which is the goal of creation, and which is made possible by Jesus Christ. Second, we know that we cannot live well apart from the grace of God. The virtues—especially the theological virtues of faith, hope, and love—are gifts that enable us to participate in God's story, and cannot be exercised without God's grace in our lives.[23] As Jonathan Wilson puts it, "Virtue is not what humans achieve, but what God enables."[24]

CHARACTER ETHICS AND PAULINE INTERPRETATION

When it comes to biblical interpretation, character ethics has recently become very influential. It has given scholars a different lens through which

22. See Meilaender, *Theory and Practice of Virtue*, x.

23. See, for example, O'Meara, "Virtues in the Theology of Thomas Aquinas." He emphasizes the source of the virtues (including love) as grace.

24. Wilson, *Gospel Virtues*, 37.

to view the ethics of the Old and New Testaments.[25] It also helps give a new perspective on how we read Scripture as a whole. Scripture tells the continuing story of all God's creation and his people.[26] It also contains the wisdom that the communities represented within it have built up over centuries as they reflected on that story. It is therefore the work of the interpreter to enable the faith community to understand its place in that narrative, and to allow itself to be transformed by it. Rather than reading solely for individual edification, we read the Scriptures together in order to become "virtuous" readers who are developing good character and so are faithful to the text.[27] The concern is not so much to find instruction and propositions for individuals to follow but to engage with Scripture in all its complexity and variety, and so, in the words of L. Gregory Jones, "to become communities of character, a holy people, who perform the Scriptures wisely and faithfully so that God may be at home in our midst"[28]

Character Ethics and Paul's Epistles

In the following chapters these ideas will be brought to bear on Rom 5:1–5. What difference does understanding faith, hope, and love as virtues make to our interpretation? What is the message of this passage when we view perseverance as a virtue, and character in terms of wisdom in community as well as personal obedience? How does understanding Paul's words in the context of the continuing narrative of God's work in the world, and our participation in that story, affect how they inform the practice of pastoral care? Before we revisit the passage, however, some important questions must be asked. We have noted some critical voices on the topic of the compatibility of character ethics with Christian theology and ethics as a whole, so we need also to ask if character ethics is an appropriate lens to use for interpreting Paul's Letter to the Romans. The dominance of Protestant biblical scholarship over the last couple centuries has meant that the idea that Paul might have had the virtues in mind has largely gone unconsidered. While the idea of the virtues was very important in ancient and medieval philosophy and theology, it fell into disuse among Protestant Christians after

25. See Brawley, *Character Ethics and the New Testament*; Carroll R. and Lapsley, *Character Ethics and the Old Testament*.

26. See Wilson, "Virtue(s)."

27. Fowl and Jones, *Reading in Communion*. See also Briggs, *Virtuous Reader*.

28. Jones, "Formed and Transformed by Scripture," 33.

the Reformation.[29] There was a strong suspicion among Protestants that to embrace the virtues was dangerously close to accepting the idea of acquiring merit and undermining the central Lutheran tenet of justification. The Protestant emphasis on divine grace and personal salvation seemed to be incompatible with what some deemed "a false sense of one's own goodness and a reliance on that goodness rather than on God's grace."[30] (This objection still troubles theologians today, as we have seen.) In addition, during the Enlightenment period, ethical thinking tended to be dominated by discussion of law and principle, and the idea of the virtues receded. In such an intellectual and theological climate, the notion that the virtues were part of Paul's thinking was either suspect or uninteresting, and so it dropped out of the interpretive picture altogether.

In recent years, however, Pauline scholars have become aware that the virtues do play a part in the apostle's worldview. Paul does think traits such as temperance and courage are significant aspects of the Christian life. In 1 Cor 6:9–10, for example, he urges temperance, patience, and prudence, among others, albeit in negative form (cf. also Rom 1:29–31; 1 Cor 5:10–11; 2 Cor 12:20). The idea of the virtues is particularly in evidence in Gal 5:19–23, where the fruits of the Spirit include perseverance and self-control. In Phil 4:8, when he is urging his readers to contemplate all that is good in order to cultivate peace in their community, he uses the term *arête*, which means "virtue" or "excellence." David E, Garland writes, "One way to fight anxiety is for Christians to focus their minds on virtues—'the real goods of virtue' as opposed to the 'false goods of pleasure.' This exhortation for them to consider whatever is true, honorable, and just is without analogy in Paul's other letters and arises from his desire to restore harmony to the community."[31]

In the same letter, Paul frequently uses the term *phroneō* (think, reason), which was commonly used in Greco-Roman philosophy to refer to practical moral reasoning. In this sense then, we can see that Paul is using language that is familiar in the Mediterranean world in which he lives and works. However, there are important differences between his thinking and philosophical schools such as the Stoics, for whom the virtues were important.[32] Here we will note only two. First, ancient thinking about the

29. See Frede, "Historic Decline of Virtue Ethics."

30. Porter, "Virtue," 205.

31. Garland, "Philippians," 253.

32. See Engberg-Petersen, *Paul and the Stoics*; Herdt ("Frailty, Fragmentation, and

virtues was concerned with what kind of attitudes would make a person a good citizen, and ultimately, what makes for a good society. For Paul, on the other hand, the primary aim is to have a greater knowledge of Christ and to share in his death and resurrection (Phil 3:10–11).[33] To that end, *phronēsis* (reasoning) is not valued for its place in the life of the *polis* (city-state), as it was for Aristotle, but for its capacity to contribute to the life of the community of believers. Most importantly, he sees the model of this mature practical reasoning in the life of Jesus (Phil 2:5).[34]

Second, in the Stoic tradition, hope for the future and an eternity are to be rejected, for the wise man concentrates on the present, "so as not to be disturbed by prospects of the future which eludes his control."[35] For Paul, however, as we have seen, the eschatological hope is central to his thinking as he looks forward to the time when God's power will be seen in all its fullness. In his thinking the virtues are important character traits for members of the community to have if they are to be able to live well as disciples of Christ in the "now and not yet."

It is also important to notice that the idea of the virtues was not only to be found among the Greeks. The virtues (although they are not called such) were to be found in the wisdom tradition of the Hebrew Scriptures. According to Ellen F. Davis, we can understand Old Testament Wisdom literature (especially the book of Proverbs, which emphasizes "wisdom and discipline, prudence and temperance") as an exegetical base for renewing a biblically informed virtue tradition. For Paul, she writes, "schooling in the virtues is simply one form of the work his ancestors called 'teach[ing] the fear of YHWH' (Ps 34:11; cf. Prov 1:7)."[36]

It is, then, quite in order for us to bring these ideas to bear on a study of our passage in Romans. The virtues, although not necessarily at the fore in Paul's writing, form part of his intellectual and cultural world, and play an important role in the fabric of his thinking.

Social Dependency") points out that Christianity was from the beginning shaped by pagan reflection on the virtues and has always been a context for thinking on the virtues and their development.

33. Harrington and Keenan, *Paul and Virtue Ethics*, 16. On the virtues in Paul see further, Kotva, *Christian Case for Virtue Ethics*, 119–31.

34. Paul frequently uses the term in Romans and also in 1 Cor 13:11; 2 Cor 13:11; Gal 5:10. See Meeks, "Man from Heaven."

35. Schumacher, "Is There Still Hope for Hope?," 215.

36. Davis, "Preserving Virtues," 184.

The idea of community, which is so important in character ethics, is also crucial for Paul. He writes as a pastor to small communities of believers, advising them how to live and work together in often hostile environments.[37] He is constantly engaged in helping his readers to build up "communities of character" that have the worship of Christ as their central aim. But what about that other major component of character ethics—narrative? It must be admitted that it is far from obvious that Paul is operating within what we would now call a narrative framework, and for years many scholars would have said that it is foreign to his thought. Recently, however, there has been a growing appreciation that story is, in fact, very important for Paul. Indeed, everything he writes to his congregations has its basis in the story of what God has done in history through the person of Jesus Christ. Not only that, he sees this story as the central part of the history of the Jewish people—from the creation of the world through the patriarchs, the exodus, the giving of the law and the teaching of the prophets.[38] When Paul writes to his congregations, then, part of his aim is to help his churches to understand where they fit into the story of God's redemption of the world.

It is easy to lose sight of how essential this story of redemption is, for rather than spell it out, Paul often assumes that his readers know the story and does not explicitly mention it.[39] Nevertheless, as we look more closely, it becomes evident that this metanarrative is very important in all of his letters, not least in the Epistle to the Romans. Paul's gospel message, and his understanding of the justification of believers, is set firmly in the story of creation, of God's dealings with the Jewish people, and of God's intervention in human history through the life, death, and resurrection of Jesus Christ. The Messiah has come, the period of the "now and the not yet" has begun, and we wait for the completion of the story at the end-times. Moreover, it is in the story of Jesus that wisdom is to be found, and not merely in the knowledge of his teachings. In fact, Jesus Christ himself is the "power of God and the wisdom of God" (1 Cor 1:24), and as we share in his

37. See Theissen, *Social Setting.* An account of the rise of scholarly interest in the earliest Christian communities, including the Pauline churches, is given in Horrell, *Social-Scientific Approaches*, 3–28.

38. For the importance of this narrative in Paul's thinking see Gorman, *Cruciformity*; Wright, *New Testament and the People of God;* Hays, *Echoes of Scripture.*

39. See the collection of essays in Longenecker, *Narrative Dynamics in Paul*; Hays, *Faith of Jesus Christ*; Fowl, *Story of Christ in the Ethics of Paul.*

continuing story, we too grow in wisdom and character. In other words, we become more Christlike.[40]

Thus, while we cannot by any means say that Paul himself thought in the same way as modern character ethicists do, we can say that essential elements of character ethics are to be found in his writings—namely the virtues, narrative, community, and wisdom. These ideas were, in fact, part of the cultural and intellectual air (both Jewish and Hellenistic) that Paul breathed. For him, however, the crucial point was that Jesus had come into the world, and everything must now be seen in the light of that.

CONCLUSION: WHAT DIFFERENCE DOES THIS MAKE?

So what difference does the choice of character ethics as a hermeneutical lens make with regard to the interpretation of Rom 5:1–5 and its use in the pastoral care of people suffering from severe depression? Most importantly, our reliance on character ethics for interpretation affects what questions we ask of the text. First, we are not so much asking it to tell us what we are *to do* as we go through the difficulties and trials of living in the "now and not yet"; rather we are asking the text what kind of people we are *to be*. In fact, given that we are concerned with the pastoral care of Christian believers, it is perhaps better to ask what kind of people Paul thinks God wants us to be in order to care for his church. It is, however, one thing to know what kind of people we should be and quite another to see how that might become a reality in our everyday lives. We will therefore also have to ask how it is that believers, with all our flaws and limitations, can be enabled to become agents of hope to those who feel hopeless.

These questions lead us to the second major effect of character ethics on interpretation. Whereas in our initial study of Rom 5:1–5 we saw hope as something we must hold on to as an act of will and obedience, we will now be considering hope as a theological virtue—a God-given distinctive characteristic of the community of believers. This move away from an emphasis on proposition, command, and obedience will have considerable implications for our use of the passage in pastoral care. Further, hope as a theological virtue cannot be understood apart from its close relatives, faith and love, and we will be obliged to reconsider their significance in Paul's argument in some depth.

40. Gorman, *Cruciformity*, 335ff.

Lastly, we will be viewing Rom 5:1–5 in light of the fact that believers are members of a community whose identity is to be found in Jesus Christ. It is the story of Christ's work in the world that informs and shapes our understanding of how God transforms us. As Stanley Hauerwas and Charles Pinches write in their book chapter on Rom 5:1–5, "The character that is capable of producing hope is that formed within the story of God's redemption in the person of Jesus Christ. Put simply, the character of Christians is possible only if Jesus has in fact been raised from the dead."[41]

But the story does not end with the resurrection. It continues, and all believers have a part to play in it. The Christian community is called, as Michael Gorman insists, to participate in the continuing narrative of Christ's work in the world, and to be transformed as it does so.[42] This too will have considerable implications for our understanding of how Christians relate to one another and of how pastoral care is to be practiced within the community of believers. With all this in mind, then, we will now return to our passage from Romans and see what difference these ideas make to our understanding of Paul's words, and how they can inform the pastoral care of for people suffering from major depression. Our principal focus will be on Paul's use of the concepts of faith, hope, and love in these verses. How does an understanding of these three as theological virtues help us in our interpretation of this text?

41. Hauerwas and Pinches, *Christians Among the Virtues*, 125.

42. Gorman, *Inhabiting the Cruciform God*.

5

Faith and the Narrative of Hope

Therefore, since we are justified by faith, we have peace with God through our Lord Jesus Christ, [2] through whom we have obtained access to this grace in which we stand; and we boast in our hope of sharing the glory of God.

—*Rom 5:1–2*

INTRODUCTION

In chapter 2, we undertook an initial exegesis of Rom 5:1–5 and considered its pastoral implications from a foundationalist perspective. It was suggested that it is possible to see hope as something that each individual believer *does*. In other words, maintaining hope, like perseverance, is an act of will. In this view, these verses are saying that believers choose to persevere in times of suffering, refusing to be crushed by the experience. They are able to do so because of faith—their knowledge of what God has done through Christ. Accordingly, the strength of character associated with good moral decision-making and living with integrity will develop, and they will be able to hold on to the hope which is theirs. Believers will be able to look back and see how God has worked in their lives during these difficult times. As they do so, helped by the Holy Spirit, they will be able to see that good can come out of their suffering and so adopt an attitude of mind that enables them to look to the future and carry on, mindful of the fact that "the best is yet to come."

From a foundationalist perspective, it is natural to see perseverance and hope as something that ought to take place in the lives of believers in times of adversity. Given what they know, believers *ought* to remember what God has done through Christ, and on that basis be able to persevere, grow in character, and so be able to hold on to the hope of the time when God's glory is revealed. Maintaining hope in suffering, in this line of thinking, is a matter of obedience in response to faith, enabled by the acknowledgement of God's love. From this perspective, too, it seems natural to conclude that pastoral carers, in order to be agents of hope, ought to encourage and exhort those who are struggling to hope to persevere, holding on to what they know. We have already noted that this view has been and can be pastorally helpful in some situations. However, for people suffering from severe depression, this approach to pastoral care could add a sense of guilt and failure to an already heavy burden. The problem is that it assumes that the person *should* be able to hold on to what he or she knows (faith) and has experienced (love) as a necessary component of the process that leads to the ability to hope. However, it is precisely this ability which is often the spiritual casualty in severe depression, and there is little or no point in exhorting someone to do what they are unable to do because of illness. Further, it is natural for both sufferers and carers to conclude that an inability to hold onto faith and the future hope in the midst of suffering is somehow to fail as a believer. From a pastoral perspective, it is hard to see how such an understanding can be a comfort to those who are finding it difficult to persevere in faith and hope.

How then, if at all, can this passage inform the pastoral care of people suffering from depression? In this chapter, we will begin to reconsider Rom 5:1–5 using insights gleaned from character ethics. Looking at our passage from the perspective of character ethics will, I suggest, yield further (different) insights for our understanding of Paul's words about suffering and hope in the life of the Christian community and how his words might inform the pastoral task of caring for people with depression. As we have seen, our change in viewpoint will mean that our attention will switch from what we ought to be *doing* as Christians to the kind of people *we are* and *should be* as we play our part in the story of Christ in the world.[1] Our first

1. Russell, "Introduction," 2: "Rightness is about what we are doing; virtue is also about how we are living."

step is to revisit the idea of faith (*pistis*), which Paul insists is the basis for our understanding of and attitude toward suffering in our lives, and its relationship to hope. What is the nature of the faith of which Paul speaks, and how does it enable us to rejoice and persevere in suffering? In particular, how does understanding faith as a theological virtue help us in our interpretation of the passage as a whole?

EXPLORING THE IDEA OF FAITH

What does Paul mean when he speaks of *pistis* ("faith")? The first and perhaps most obvious way to understand it is in terms of belief. For example, Paul says in Rom 4:25 that it is because we believe in the proposition that God raised Jesus Christ from the dead for the justification of humanity that we now have access to God's grace, and share the hope of one day sharing in the revealed glory of Christ. On the basis of this knowledge, our attitude toward suffering is changed and we are able to see it as a medium for hope. It is because of the belief that God has acted in Christ that we are able to persevere in suffering, develop strength of character, and so be able to hold on to hope for the future.

Besides belief, however, Paul's appeal to the story of Abraham as an example of one whose righteousness was on the basis of faith also suggests that the idea of trust is an important element of *pistis*. Abraham not only believed what God had said; he also lived his life as one who trusted that what God had said would come to pass. In both senses, Abraham's faith was a matter of choice and will, and therefore of obedience. We also, like Abraham, choose to trust that God has acted in history in the person of Jesus Christ, and that he continues to act by means of the Holy Spirit.[2] This continuing trust gives us the rationale for everyday living, and the basis for maintaining hope.

But is an active choice to believe and trust all that Paul has in mind when he speaks of *pistis*? If so, this raises a problem, for as the personal accounts we presented in chapter 2 attest, in severe depression previous certainties can be eroded or even lost. The sense of abandonment of which John Colwell speaks in *Why Have You Forsaken Me?*, for example, is hardly conducive to being able to maintain belief and trust in God.

2. For a study of Paul's understanding of faith see Gupta, *Paul and the Language of Faith*.

Faith as a Virtue

The remarks above are not intended to undermine the importance of the understanding of faith in terms of assent and trust. This remains the most natural and primary way of understanding the place of faith in the Christian life. According to Thomas Aquinas, "To believe is an act of mind assenting to divine truth by virtue of the command of the will as this is moved by God through grace; in this way the act stands under the control of the free will, and is directed towards God."[3]

Christians are required to give intellectual assent to "divine truth," and they do so as an act of will. But God has not only provided the object of our belief. In Aquinas's terms, faith, as one of the theological virtues, is infused in the believer: that is, God also gives us the ability to believe, and to sustain that belief. As with all the virtues, however, we must exercise or practice this gift of faith by an act of the will. In other words, there is a sense in which we must consciously and deliberately choose to believe and continue to do so.[4]

However, the Christian life is much more than assent or adherence to a proposition. As Keith Clements insists, Christian faith is based on a relationship with God, and our lives and actions are shaped by that relationship.[5] Moreover, from the perspective of Christian character ethics, faith (like all the virtues) is not merely concerned with what we know, but with the kind of people we are and want to be. The relationship is based on knowledge, certainly, but it is sustained both by our continued reliance on God's faithfulness to us (trust) and our faithful commitment to God (fidelity). Avery Dulles, a Jesuit theologian, writes, "Faith, without ceasing to be an assent of the mind, involves a trusting commitment of the whole person to God who reveals, together with fidelity and obedience to the saving message."[6]

Besides intellectual assent, and trust in God's character, we must also live lives of faithful response. We too must be faithful as God himself is faithful. But what does it mean to live faithful, trusting lives? From a character-ethics perspective, the answer to that question is to be found in the

3. Thomas Aquinas, *Summa Theologica*, I-II,2.9.

4. On Thomas Aquinas, see Harrington and Keenan *Paul and Virtue Ethics*, 83–89.

5. See also Clements, *Faith*, 7: Christian faith has as its innermost quality "personal relationship to God in Christ."

6. Dulles, "Faith and Revelation," 107.

Christian story. Jesus is the prime example of one whose life is oriented to God and his will for the world. In the gospels we read of his faithfulness and obedience to God's purposes. We also learn what faithfulness entails from Jesus' own teaching, much of which is in the form of story. From this teaching we learn of the values (or virtues) that are important for people who profess to be Christ's faithful followers—compassion, mercy, and justice, for example—and that influence our actions and ethical decision-making.

According to character ethics, faith as a theological virtue is a God-given character trait that informs our whole lives. It entails not only belief, and trusting in God's faithfulness to his purposes, but also a desire to live faithfully in the way that Christ did. Moreover, as Jonathan Wilson notes, faithful people are transformed into the likeness of Christ (2 Cor 3:18; Rom 8:29; Phil 3:21): "Faith is the transformation of everything we are as persons. It is the creation of a new being in Jesus Christ by the power of the Holy Spirit."[7]

As we offer our wills and desires to God, we are opening ourselves up to be changed and conformed to God's character. At every stage, we are aware that it is through grace that we are able to continue in belief, trust, and faithfulness. Crucially, the gift of faith is not to be seen in solely individualistic terms—it can only be exercised as part of the Spirit-filled community of believers, the body of Christ.[8] The transformation of which Wilson speaks takes place in communities in which we worship together and learn from one another.

From this discussion, we may suggest that when Paul speaks of faith he is thinking in terms of belief, trust, and faithful response. The faith that justifies believers and gives them peace with God, access to grace, and hope for the future rests on believing in what God has done and continuing to trust in his faithfulness to us. We have also suggested, influenced by character ethics, that faith is to be understood in terms of faithfulness or fidelity. Christians are to be characterized by fidelity—living faithful, obedient lives in response to what God has done and continues to do in the world—and they learn how to live with fidelity from the story of Jesus' life. When faith in all these senses is presented as a theological virtue, we see that it is to be understood primarily as a gift from God rather than as a trait that we can exhibit under our own strength.

7. Wilson, *Gospel Virtues*, 61.

8. Wilson, *Gospel Virtues*, 68.

THE MEANING OF FAITH IN PAUL

Before we return to Rom 5:1–5 and see how this broadened understanding of faith helps us grasp Paul's teaching here on the relationship between suffering and hope, a question needs to be addressed. Is this understanding of faith compatible with Paul's thinking? Over many decades, the Lutheran idea of *sola fide*—the idea that our salvation comes about solely as a result of a human response of belief and trust in what God has done through Jesus Christ—has been highly influential among biblical scholars. This has meant that when Paul speaks of faith, he has been understood as referring to belief and trust on the part of the individual. Here, however, we have been suggesting that God gives us a gift that enables us to be faithful. Is such a view not at risk of lessening the importance of an obedient response to God's grace on our part? Recently, a line of thinking has developed among some scholars that opens up the possibility that Paul might have a much broader notion of faith than previously understood.

We have seen that Paul considers the believer's relationship with God to be grounded in faith. Earlier in the letter, he has argued that humanity has fallen into sin, and has declared that "all have sinned and fall short of the glory of God" (3:23). Humanity as a whole is far from being the way God wants it to be. However, God has provided a way out of this parlous state. Righteousness before God, Paul says in 3:22, is to be found *dia pisteōs Iēsou Christou*, and this is the case for all human beings, whether they come from a Jewish or Gentile background. We must now explore what this phrase, which is usually translated as "faith in Jesus Christ," might mean. What does Paul mean when he speaks of faith here?

Paul uses the phrase *pistis Christou* in various places in his letters. For instance, in Rom 3, besides the example we have already noted, he says that God justifies *ek pisteōs Iēsou* (Rom 3:26). We find the same notion in Galatians (Gal 2:15–16 and 3:21–22), while in Philippians 3:8–9 the apostle speaks of righteousness *dia* (through) *pisteōs Christou*. Traditionally, the phrase *pistis Christou* has been translated as "faith in Christ" and these passages taken to mean that justification for individuals is brought about by the person's response of belief and trust in the work of Jesus. For example, as we have seen, when Paul says in Rom 3:21–22 that the righteousness of God has been manifested apart from the law, he qualifies this statement with the phrase *dia pisteōs Iēsou Christou*. The NRSV translates:

> But now, apart from law, the righteousness of God has been disclosed, and is attested by the law and the prophets, the righteousness of God through faith in Jesus Christ for all who believe.

On this understanding (which takes the Greek construction as an objective genitive), Paul is saying that men and women are able to become righteous before God by means of their belief and trust in the person and work of Jesus Christ. Those who believe in Jesus Christ are able to understand and apprehend the righteousness of God.

However, it is also possible to understand the Greek construction as a subjective genitive. This means that we can translate *dia pisteōs Iesou Christou* as "through (the) faith of Jesus Christ." In this case, Paul is saying that God's righteousness was revealed through Jesus Christ's *faithfulness* to God's purposes and to the task he had to carry out as the means by which the righteousness of God was revealed to the world. Understood this way, Rom 3:22 is saying that the righteousness of God was revealed or brought about through the faithful work of Jesus Christ.

The idea that the phrase *pistis christou* may refer to Jesus' own faithfulness to God's purposes has caused not a little controversy among Pauline scholars.[9] This very complex debate, which involves both grammatical and theological considerations, continues and no doubt will do for some time. Opposition to the less traditional reading comes from those who worry about the idea that Jesus' faithfulness has something to do with the justification of believers; they argue that the subjective-genitive reading reduces the emphasis on the need for responding to the work of Christ in faith. In this view, when Paul refers to faith he is referring to an entirely human response of faith in Christ as opposed to "works of the law." In other words, it reduces our responsibility as hearers of the gospel.

However, in response, we might point out that had Jesus been unfaithful to God's purposes, had he avoided death at the hands of sinful humanity, there would have been no resurrection, and therefore no grounds for our hope. It is because of Jesus' faithfulness to God's purposes that the way was opened up for God's righteousness to be revealed to all men and women, and for humanity to be justified and have access to God. It is therefore quite in order to say that in Paul's thinking Christ's faithfulness has an important part to play in our justification, without denying that there is a responsibility for men and women to respond by believing, trusting, and living faithful lives.

9. On the often fraught debate regarding the translation of the phrase *pistis christou* in Paul, see Bird and Sprinkle, *Faith of Jesus Christ*.

Faith and the Narrative of Christ

The question for us now is how this idea of Christ's faithfulness in Paul's thought relates to our hermeneutic informed by character ethics, and our understanding of faith as a virtue. The key lies in the idea of narrative, which, as we have already noted, is important in character ethics. Everything that we do as believers is informed by the story of God's work through Christ. In their book *Resident Aliens*, Stanley Hauerwas and William Willimon write, "Christian ethics depends upon the Christian story. Christian ethics makes no sense apart from the recognition that we are also on an adventuresome journey which requires a peculiar set of virtues."[10]

It is the Christian story, then, that forms the basis of our faith. We assent to it intellectually, and we seek to be faithful to that story, by means of the virtues. However, Scripture makes it clear that the story of God's work in the world is not yet finished, and Christians have a part to play in the continuing narrative. We continue to trust in God and live faithful lives, and as we do so, we participate in the work of God. The basis of such lives is the gift (or virtue) or faith. By means of this gift we are able to give assent to the story and to trust in God's purposes for his world. Moreover, we are enabled to take responsibility and be faithful to God's purposes for this world, just as Christ himself was faithful.[11]

In his book *Cruciformity: Paul's Narrative Spirituality of the Cross*, Michael J. Gorman argues that narrative is central to Paul's thinking. For Gorman, the term "the faith of Christ" is a "'summary allusion'" to the story of "'Jesus' fidelity in carrying out his mission' vis-à-vis God and us, the focus and epitome being the cross."[12] Accordingly, the Christian life is "a dynamic correspondence in daily life to the strange story of Christ crucified as the primary way of experiencing the love and grace of God."[13]

10. Hauerwas and Willimon, *Resident Aliens*, 63.

11. Hauerwas, *Peaceable Kingdom*, 39. "Agency," he says, "encapsulates our sense that we are responsible for what we are." Character is the "qualification or determination of our self-agency, formed by our having certain intentions (and beliefs) rather than others. Our character is not merely the result of our choices, but rather the form our agency takes through our beliefs and intentions. So understood, the idea of agency helps us to see that our character is not a surface manifestation of some deeper reality called the 'self.' We are our characters."

12. Gorman *Cruciformity*, 120. Gorman is referring to Richard B. Hays's article, "PISTIS CHRISTOU and Pauline Theology," 37.

13. Gorman, *Cruciformity*, 5.

For the believer, faith entails an intellectual assent to the gospel, trust and confidence in God, and faithful living.

Scripture provides narratives of many whose lives may be described as faithful, to a greater or lesser extent. For Paul, Abraham is a particularly good example. The patriarch trusted God's word to him and was faithful: his flaws notwithstanding, he was obedient and loyal to God throughout his life. Abraham's faith, Paul says, "was reckoned to him as righteousness" (Rom 4:3). However, as Gorman notes, for Paul, Jesus is the far greater, indeed the perfect example of faithful living, and we should try to imitate him. When Paul writes to the Philippians, he tells them that they should have the same mindset as Christ, who gave up all his privileges as God's son, came to earth and took the form of a slave (Phil 2:1–11). Such humility is to be a distinctive excellence of the Christian community. But there are further implications: believers not only follow Christ's example but share in Jesus' faithfulness: "To enter into relationship with this God," Gorman writes, "is to identify fully, both cognitively and existentially (in *head* and in *heart*) with the cross and resurrection of Jesus."[14] The Christian life of faith, then, means to follow Christ's example and to share in his sufferings. In fact, in so doing, believers actually participate in the work of God. Josef Pieper puts it this way, "for the believer there is once more the experience that he, in accepting the message of the self-revealing God, actually partakes of the divine life therein announced."[15]

IMPLICATIONS FOR THE UNDERSTANDING OF *PISTIS* IN ROMANS 5:1–5

Having seen that this broader understanding of faith and its relationship to the narrative of Scripture is compatible with Paul's thinking, we can now return to considering in some depth the nature of the faith which justifies, gives believers peace with God, and forms the basis of our hope of sharing in the glory of God. The Christian community is made up of people who have been made righteous before God by means of faith. This "distinctive excellence" of faith refers to belief in what God has done through Christ, continuing trust in the divine promise of faithful presence and ultimate vindication, and faithful living in response. Faith entails belief in what God has done, trust that God is faithful in the present and that he will one day

14. Gorman, *Cruciformity*, 140.

15. Pieper, *Faith, Hope, Love*, 85.

redeem his creation. It also entails an active response from us—imitation of the faithfulness of Christ. Focused on God, rather than ourselves, our faith is gift and response—not a personal achievement.

It is because they are given the gift of faith (in its broadest sense of assent, trust, and faithfulness) that believers can say that they have peace with God and stand in grace. As Hans Urs von Balthasar writes, "[Faith] is the grace which comes to us in God's self-giving and enables us to give ourselves to him in return."[16]

This grace is ours through a process of "infusion." As we saw in our discussion of the virtues, this is crucial to our development of character, as God works in us to transform our lives. Faith is therefore much more than the mere knowledge that one stands in God's grace, or "the acceptance of this unearned honor," as Jewett suggests.[17] It is much more than clinging to a memory of something that has happened in the past. Rather, we are believing, trusting, and faithful people, and these God-given characteristics enable us to shoulder the responsibility of discipleship. They are qualities of mind distinctive to God's people, and because we have these distinctives we are able to participate in God's continuing story and so rejoice, no matter what our circumstances, and hope for the future.

Moreover, the disciplines of believing, trusting, and living faithfully are carried out in community—with others whose lives are given meaning because of their imitation of and sharing in Christ's own faithfulness as the Son of God.[18] This is not to deny the importance of the faith of the individual, but it is to say that faith is dangerously truncated if it is seen as significant only for the salvation or benefit of the individual concerned. In fact, the "distinctive excellence" of faith means that the community must be, by its very nature, outward looking. The development of the virtues must, as Colin Gunton notes, be "exocentric." They must be grounded in our faith in God and mediated by our relationship to God, and are given to us for the "sake of the world."[19] The community cannot be self-absorbed. Strengthened by the Holy Spirit, who helps us in our weakness, we are enabled to persevere and grow as we play our part in the unfinished story of God's intervention in the world.

16. Von Balthasar, *Prayer*, 36.

17. So Jewett, *Romans*, 333.

18. For the view that faith for Paul is both individual and communal see Dunson, "Faith in Romans."

19. Gunton, "Church as a School of Virtue?," 228–29.

FAITH, SUFFERING, AND HOPE

How does this deeper understanding of faith, influenced by character ethics and the idea of the virtues, affect our understanding of the relationship between faith, suffering, and hope? First, when faith is understood in terms of virtue, a gift from God rather than primarily in terms of obedience and will, practicing perseverance (another virtue) in suffering may be understood as something believers can do because of the kind of people we are. We are able to persevere because of who we are by God's grace—believing, trusting, and loyal people. Certainly, we have agency in this (we have choice), but when we come to understand the nature the gift that we have been given, we realize that we have been given the means to maintain our lives of faith, so the temptation to try to act on our own wills is considerably reduced. The basis for our ability to persevere in suffering, then, is a divine gift. No wonder Paul links suffering, rejoicing, and hope!

Second, the fact that *pistis* entails our faithfulness—the model for which is Christ's own faithfulness in suffering—means that we can make sense of our own suffering in the context of our new identity as his disciples. Our suffering is part of our experience on the journey of faith, in which we are transformed and become more Christlike. We will explore this idea further in the next chapter, but here we note that when we suffer, we endure because we are disciples of Christ, and as we do so we grow in character and Christlikeness. The concepts of perseverance and developing character entail the ideas of journey, growth, and transformation. The relationship that is central to our faith is dynamic, not static, and entails our growth in wisdom and maturity. Crucially, our life of faith is not a solo experience: We are part of a community of faithful people who share in Christ's sufferings together, able to support one another and to learn from one another.

Third, faith means our suffering in this life is given meaning, for in our faithfulness we are identifying with and sharing in Christ's suffering. Christians understand their lives to be part of the narrative of God's intervention in history. Suffering is thus given new significance; we are playing our part in the story of Christ. Our faithful response is to obey the teachings of Christ and to imitate the way he lived, and even to embrace suffering as the way God works to change the world. In fact, Paul makes our sharing in the eschatological hope contingent on this: We have to suffer with Christ in order to share in his inheritance of universal sovereignty (Rom 8:17–25).

And in the same way that Christ's sufferings were for the sake of the world, so, somehow, our suffering will have a part to play in God's purposes for humanity.

The Christian life, lived in the "now and not yet," is a school in which "our faith begins to learn the meaning of faithfulness."[20] As people who have a new identity in Christ (*en Christō*), and who are no longer under the power of sin (6:2), the expectation is of transformation (even though we may have some battles along the way). We develop and grow and understand the implications of our belief more deeply, learn how to trust more fully and discover more of what it means to be faithful. Therefore, we must not try to deny our sufferings, for to do so would be to deny our relationship with Christ, who suffered for all humanity. Likewise, our sufferings are not merely for our own sakes but are, in some way, for others too. We do not endure in order to grow in virtue, or seek character for its own sake; we persevere because we have been given the gift of faith.

FAITH, DEPRESSION, AND PASTORAL CARE

The faith at the basis of the Christian's ability to rejoice and persevere in their suffering, then, is much more than a matter of willful obedience on the part of an individual. In fact, having been given the gift of faith, believers have been given the means by which they can endure and see significance in their experience. For they are playing their part in the continuing story of Christ in the world. In the next chapter, we will explore further the idea of hope as a theological virtue, and what this means with regard to the role of pastoral carers as agents of hope. Here, however, we may make some preliminary remarks.

When faith is understood in terms of something that believers ought to do, the implication is that we must continually choose to cling to the proposition or idea in which we believe and trust. Similarly, if we are to be faithful, we must find the strength to be so in ourselves, as a matter of will. While this is something which many Christians may be able to do in the normal run of things, this concept of faith can be problematic for people experiencing extreme suffering, and we are again confronted with the difficulty that those who suffer from depression may feel unable to hold on to their faith. Indeed, people with depression are often deeply distressed by their lack of belief and their inability to trust and be faithful, and chastise themselves for this.

20. Meilaender, *Faith and Faithfulness*, 116.

Two main aspects of character ethics help to mitigate these difficulties. First, the fact that faith is not simply something that one does, but is a gift given to us by God, means that we are people whose lives are characterized by faith. In pastoral perspective then, the depressed believer is not to be seen as disobedient, but as temporarily, as a result of illness, unable to exercise the gift which they have been given. Second, character ethics helps us to see faith not so much as an individual responsibility (although this is not discounted altogether) as a corporate characteristic of the community of followers of Jesus. So, when one of its number no longer feels able to believe, trust, or be faithful, the community bears the burden for them as it groans together awaiting redemption at the end-times (Rom 8:22–24). Pastoral care becomes a matter of support rather than instruction and rebuke. Although exhortation is not necessarily ruled out, we gather round, and do not reject—for we are all on the same journey, with the same end in view.

CONCLUSION

In this chapter, as part of our exploration of character ethics as a hermeneutical lens through which to view Paul's words on suffering and hope in Rom 5:1–5, we have been exploring the idea of faith as a theological virtue. Drawing on recent Pauline scholarship with regard to the understanding of *pistis* in Paul, we have seen that this gives us a much broader and deeper understanding of the nature of faith as a way of being, rather than merely a matter of assent to a proposition. Christians are believing, trusting, and faithful people, who share in the sufferings of Christ and are transformed into his likeness as they do so. We have seen too that this faith is given to us as a grace from God, and so when it comes to the experience of suffering, we already have been given all that we need to endure. Already we have been able to draw some pastoral implications of this understanding with regard to the care of people suffering from depression. We have moved away from the idea that the struggles with faith that often accompany depression represent disobedience and failure, and toward the idea that the depressed believer (because of illness) is unable to use the gift that has been given. We have also moved away from the idea that Paul's words imply a need to correct spiritual failure. In the next chapter, we will consider the link between suffering and hope in Rom 5:1–5 in greater detail, and explore what it means to understand hope as a theological virtue.

6

A Hopeful Community

And not only that, but we also boast in our sufferings, knowing that suffering produces endurance, and endurance produces character, and character produces hope.

—*Rom 5:3–4*

Hope deferred makes the heart sick,
but a desire fulfilled is a tree of life.

—*Prov 13:12*

ROMANS 5:3–4 THROUGH THE LENS OF CHARACTER ETHICS

Having considered the idea of faith as a gift from God in Rom 5:1–2, and having begun to note the difference a hermeneutic informed by character ethics makes with regard to the use of our text in the pastoral care of people with depression, we will now return to the sequence of thought in verses 3–4. We will see that adopting this approach will require us to reconsider our understanding of perseverance, the nature of Christian character, and, indeed, of hope itself. We have noted that in 5:1–2 Paul states that because of God's action in the past and our response of faith (in the sense of belief, trust, and faithfulness), our current lives are marked by peace with God and access to divine grace. In other words, those who believe that God has acted in Jesus Christ and who respond with trust and faithfulness are no longer struggling against divine purposes. With regard to the future, they rejoice because they have the "hope . . . of the glory of God" being revealed in all its fullness. God's intervention in history through the person of Christ, and his gift of faith to believers (in its broadest sense) brings about an entirely new view of past, present, and future.

Given this teaching about grace and justification, it might be tempting to think that the life of the believer should be smooth sailing and trouble free. If any such misunderstanding has arisen in Rome, Paul is keen to dispel it. Believers may have been given "incongruous grace,"[1] but this does not exempt them from suffering. Later in the letter, as we have already noted, Paul will explain that suffering is a necessary part of the Christian life (8:17). The future hope of sharing in the glory of God is in fact conditional upon sharing in the sufferings of Christ. In verse 3 of chapter 5 he begins to explore the idea of hope by making the startling and, for us today, counterintuitive claim that persevering in suffering, for believers, is directly related to the future hope we have. Not only that, but suffering has a crucial part to play in the development of our ability to sustain that hope in our everyday lives—in the present time. Our task in this chapter is to try to understand how this might be so. In order to do this, we will revisit the sequence of thought in verses 3–4. As we will see, when the concepts of perseverance and hope are viewed as virtues which are crucial in the development of character, they take on quite a different color from that in our initial investigation in chapter 3. We will now reconsider each of the terms in turn, paying particular attention to the nature of hope. What kind of people does God want believers to be when suffering comes? What does it mean to say that hope, as a theological virtue, is a distinctive excellence of the Christian community? How does this inform our understanding of the place of suffering in the Christian life and our pastoral response to those who feel hopeless?

Perseverance

At first sight the idea of perseverance in suffering does not really change much when viewed from the perspective of character ethics. Perseverance

1. Barclay, *Paul and the Gift*.

remains something that we do—there is a sense in which it is an active, conscious choice, strengthened by the knowledge of what God has done in Christ. However, in the perspective of character ethics, perseverance becomes not so much an act of the will (although this aspect is not totally lost) as something for which God has given us capacity. Thus, perseverance is no longer solely a matter of gritting our teeth and getting on with things. We already have the ability to learn and practice it, and as we do so we become better able to withstand the suffering that comes our way. It is helpful to remember, too, that as a virtue, perseverance is the mean between two extremes. Too little perseverance will result in collapsing under the strain of our experience of suffering. Too much perseverance and we might find that we are causing ourselves (and possibly others) unnecessary suffering—for example, by failing to try to find a solution for our situation or a way to ameliorate it. For Christians, then, the point is that we must be reliant on God to enable us to persevere in a sensible and wise way.

Of course, persevering in suffering is something that all human beings in every culture and age can do, but in the context of this passage, our ability to persevere cannot be divorced from the Christian narrative of which we are a part. It rests on the fact that God has acted in history through Christ's death and resurrection, and continues to act through the Holy Spirit. It rests, too, on the reality that those who respond in faith enjoy a profound change in their relationship with God: they are no longer at odds with the divine will but are standing in a state of grace. Moreover, they are now participating in the continuing story of Christ's work in the world. All this has eternal significance in the life of the believer. It is because of this that we are enabled to withstand the trials that face us. Ultimately, we have nothing to fear. As Stanley Hauerwas and Charles Pinches remind us, "Christians can endure because through Christ they have been given power over death and all the forms of victimization that trade on it. The ultimate power of Christ is the victory over death that makes possible the endurance of suffering: we can endure because we have confidence that though our enemies may kill us they cannot determine the meaning of our death."[2]

For Christians, the ability to persevere in suffering, therefore, stems from the profound sense of meaning and the transformative power that being part of God's story provides. In other words, Christians do not persevere in a moral or theological vacuum, but in the conscious knowledge of the continuing story of God's activity in human history—the story which

2. Hauerwas and Pinches, *Christians Among the Virtues*, 123.

gives meaning to all that they do, and in which they have an active role to play.

Character

Viewing the passage through this lens also requires that we revisit what we mean when we speak of character. In chapter 3, we spoke of Christian character as moral strength—the kind of resilience that sees us through bad times. The suggestion was that as we persevere, we build up the kind of resilience and moral courage that enable us to make good decisions and do what is right when difficulties arise. In this view, Christian character is the willingness to do what God requires of us, the desire to do what God commands. Adopting a character-ethics perspective provides us with some fresh insights.

The desire to do God's will is part and parcel of our new identity in Christ. But we are still in the "now and not yet," and prone to making mistakes and even "falling away." It is, of course, indicative of the nature of God's grace that he is able repeatedly to restore us. This has led some to characterize the Christian life in terms of repeated falling away and returning to God.[3] There are, however, problems with this view of Christian life, which Gilbert Meilaender has described as a "going back and forth, back and forth," ultimately going nowhere. He writes, "We might think of the Christian life as a dialogue, with the Christian caught between the two voices with which God speaks: the demanding voice of law and the accepting voice of gospel. Life is experienced as a dialogue between these two divine verdicts, and within human history one cannot escape that dialogue or progress beyond it."[4]

As Hauerwas and Pinches point out in their study of Rom 5:1–5, this very static view of Christian experience does not seem to have room for the idea of growth and maturity.[5] A character-ethics perspective moves us toward a view of Christian character in which we learn from our mistakes and grow in wisdom. We are, as the philosopher Thomas Aquinas has famously described it, *homo viator*: Christian life is a journey of learning and

3. Barth, *Church Dogmatics*, 644–45 (cited in Hauerwas and Pinches, *Christians Among the Virtues*, 115).

4. Meilaender, *Limits of Love*, 34–5.

5. For all this see Hauerwas and Pinches, *Christians Among the Virtues*, 113–28.

growth in moral and spiritual stature.[6] For Hauerwas, to say that a person has "character" is to say that he or she has "integrity, incorruptibility and consistency."[7] Moral stature of this sort is not gained passively, but comes about through conscious choices that we make in the midst of the circumstances and difficulties of our lives, in our responses to what happens to us. Indeed, Lisa Sowle Cahill suggests that this idea of character contains within it an element of struggle: "Character carries an overtone of *resistance to* and *steadfastness against* threatening powers or forces against which the strong must stand firm."[8]

As we engage in this resistance, guided by the stories and wisdom of Scripture, we are increasingly able to discern what is good and right and to work toward it, recognizing the enemies of the good and the right, and working against them. Thus, character means not just resilience but an increasing wisdom that enables good choices to be made in the light of experience. In spiritual terms, this means that we become more Christlike as we follow his example and play our part in his story. We develop the characteristics of Christ himself—in particular his humility and sacrificial love (Phil 2:5–11). So it is that as we persevere, we are continually being transformed "by the renewing of [our] minds" (Rom 12:1). As we persevere, and reflect on our experience, we come to an ever-greater appreciation of the significance of our faith, a deeper understanding of our relationship with God and, transformation of our minds as God works in our lives. Our tested characters develop an increasing appreciation of the nature of God's faithfulness and the need for our own faithful response.

Lastly, for Western Christians at least, there is always a temptation to think of character only in individualistic terms, seeing our task as Christians as holding on to faith and drawing ever closer to God. However, considering the passage from the perspective of character ethics provides a useful corrective to this. It is certainly always important that we ask how we as individuals can be faithful Christians. But a preoccupation with personal piety and morality runs the risk of neglecting the Christian community as a whole. As we have seen, the virtues are practiced not for our own benefit primarily but for the sake of the community, and indeed humanity as a whole. In fact, good character cannot be cultivated in isolation, and the reason to seek it is not simply to ensure that we are personally right before

6. This idea is explored in full by Marcel in *Homo Viator*, 1951.

7. Hauerwas, *Character and the Christian Life*, 15.

8. Cahill, "Christian Character."

God but so that our communities can flourish, and the church fulfils its purpose as a distinctive entity in the world.

Hope

In our initial exploration of Rom 5:1–5 we saw that hope may be considered an attitude of mind that is based on the intellectual acceptance of certain propositions, which we call faith. In this case, the proposition is that God has intervened in history through the person of Jesus Christ. We saw too that for Paul, hope has a specific content, namely that believers will one day share in the glory of God: on that day, "creation itself will be set free from its bondage to decay and will obtain the freedom of the glory of the children of God" (Rom 8:20). Thus, according to our first interpretation hope was understood as an expectation of something that will happen in the future, something that is as yet not seen (Rom 8:24). So when suffering comes, people of faith have something to look forward to that is quite different from their current experience.

On this understanding, then, the hope of which Paul speaks is, in psychological terms, the ability to see that things can be, and indeed will be, better than they are now. It is this which sustains believers through difficult times. Further, our foundationalist interpretation of the passage, which detected an implicit imperative in Paul's words, suggested that when believers experience suffering, they ought to be able, on the basis of what they know and by exercising resolve, to adopt a hopeful attitude of mind in which they cling to the promise of better things in the future. That is to say, the onus is on the individual to be hopeful as a matter of obedience; it is something that he or she ought to be able to do on the basis of the faith (i.e., the knowledge) that they have.

This idea of the nature of hope is not uncommon. In an article posted on the website of *Sojourners* magazine, for example, Jim Wallis writes "Hope is not just feeling, but decision. Hope is our vocation and identity as the people of God."[9] Wallis argues that Christians need to be hopeful in the face of the many injustices in the world such as human trafficking, gender-based violence, and terrorism, and he urges his readers to have hope in order to combat the hatred in the world. Now, as we have already noted, there is no doubt that this idea has been and continues to be encouraging and comforting to many people in many situations. However, it is hard to

9. Wallis, "Way of Hope."

see how the injunction to be hopeful might be of any help when one has lost the ability to hope because of severe depression.

When hope is understood as a theological virtue (in Thomas Aquinas's terms), however, the emphasis changes. As we saw in the discussion of faith, there is less stress on an act of human will and obedience, and more on the idea of acceptance and use of a gift from God. In this view, Christians are hopeful people because we have been given the gift of hope. We do not have to hold on to the expectation of a better future as if all depended on our efforts. What we must do is exercise the gift of hopefulness as we make our journey toward the time when God will be all in all. We are living in a time when God has already revealed this hope to us in the person and work of Jesus Christ. And because Christ's work has inaugurated a new age, we live in the "now and not yet" as we wait for the final revelation. As Josef Pieper says, "the only answer that corresponds to man's existential situation is hope. The virtue of hope is pre-eminently the virtue of the *status viatoris*; it is the proper virtue of the 'not yet.'"[10]

In this understanding, we note first of all, Christian hope becomes not only an expectation that something will happen in the future; it is a gift that we exercise in the here and now as we continue on the journey. Through this hope, according to Thomas Aquinas, we trust that with divine assistance we will attain the infinite good—eternal enjoyment of God.[11]

Second, in accordance with our view of hope as a theological virtue, it is useful to understand hope as the mean between the extremes of triumphalism (sometimes called presumption) and despair. According to Harrington and Keenan, "Despair means that the wayfarer no longer believes that the journey is doable. Presumption means that the journey is doable, but that we do not need to rely on God. In neither vice do we in fact rely on God. God is beyond our needs for the journey."[12]

The gift of hope, then, is given to us to enable us to continue on the journey, all the while relying on God to help us. However, the journey through the "now and not yet" is a difficult one that is fraught with

10. Pieper *Faith, Hope, Love*, 98.

11. *Summa Theologica*, II-II.17.1–2. Most philosophers do not consider hope to be a virtue. For example, Comte-Sponville (*Short Treatise on the Great Virtues*, 287) has difficulty with the idea of hope as a virtue because it "has no plausible object, other than God, in whom I do not believe." For the Christian, of course, God *is* the plausible object of hope. The concept of God and one's relationship with him are what give life meaning and reason for living.

12. Harrington and Keenan, *Paul and Virtue Ethics*, 104–5.

temptations and risks. On the one hand, there is the temptation to despair, to think that we will never be able to get to the end of the journey, and on the other hand there is temptation to think that we are able to carry on without God—in other words, that we do not need him at all. The mean between these two extremes is a realistic view both of our own abilities in avoiding these temptations and of our relationship to God. This in turn has the rather paradoxical outcome that we are encouraged to depend all the more on God rather than on our own resources.

Third, as our exploration of character ethics teaches us to expect, this gift of hope is not only for our own individual emotional well-being but for the benefit of the community as a whole. If the virtues are excellences that speak of the power of something to fulfil its purpose, hope is given to enable the Christian community to do precisely that—to worship God, to bear witness to him and to the story of his intervention in history through Christ. As Gabriel Marcel notes, "there can be no hope which does not constitute itself through a we and for a we . . . all hope is at bottom choral."[13]

To say that we have the virtue of hope, therefore, is to say that we have been given a gift that will drive us toward the good in our Christian lives, and that when exercised (for it must be exercised), enables our Christian communities to thrive. Thus, for the Christian, hope can only make sense in relation to the community, for it cannot be exercised in isolation from the Christian community and its teaching. Hoping, then, is not something that we do alone and for ourselves only: we exercise the gift for the sake of others.

This brings us to the fourth aspect of hope—its place in the present. While it is true to say that Christian hope is future oriented and we look forward to the day when God will be seen in all his glory and we will be revealed as his sons and daughters, it is also crucial to see that hope exists in the here and now. For if we limit our understanding of hope to something that refers only to the future, we will find ourselves cut off from present reality. The belief that the content of hope is limited to the future is a dangerous way to think, for it can put us above the groaning of creation and render us unable to feel compassion for our fellow creatures. If we focus only on what is to come, we will devalue the present, reducing our hope to what Daniel Migliore calls a "cheap optimism" that "fails to share in the present agony of the world."[14] We can be tempted to think that our own present suffering is

13. Marcel, *Tragic Wisdom and Beyond*, 143.

14. Migliore, *Faith Seeking Understanding*, 356.

of no significance or that the suffering of others, whether within or outside the Christian community, is of no concern to us.

The problem is that if hope is limited to the idea of a better future, it becomes little more than a source of psychological comfort: the thought of what is to come merely makes us feel better in the present. But as Jürgen Moltmann insists, the eschatological hope is not intended for us to become self-righteous and complacent in the present, unconcerned for the suffering in the world. Rather, our expectation of future glory is in fact an awareness of the way things can be and should be. It is in the light of this awareness that the suffering of the present time is thrown into sharp relief and we see that we must do something to bring about change. Moltmann puts it this way: "Faith, wherever it develops into hope, causes not rest but unrest, not patience but impatience. It does not calm the unquiet heart, but is itself this unquiet heart in man. Those who hope in Christ can no longer put up with reality as it is, but begin to suffer under it, to contradict it. Peace with God means conflict with the world, for the goad of the promised future stabs inexorably into the flesh of every unfulfilled present."[15]

When we consider the future hope we see the brokenness of the world in a way we did not before, recognizing the need to respond to the suffering of others. We realize that our part in the story of Christ is to bring healing and transformation into the broken world in the here and now. As Moltmann says, Christian hope is "forward looking and forward moving, and therefore also revolutionizing and transforming the present."[16] To exercise the gift of hope, then, is to serve the broken and needy of this world and to contribute to the transformation of their lives and our own.

As we persevere in suffering, then, we grow in maturity and wisdom and are enabled to exercise the gift of hope that we have been given. We are increasingly enabled, not only to hold on to what we know of what the future will entail, but to understand how it is that expectation informs our lives in the here and now, and how best to live in response to it—that is to say, to be a hopeful people.

A DEEPER, RICHER INTERPRETATION

How does all this help us to understand the relationship between suffering and hope? First, we have seen that from the perspective of character ethics,

15. Moltmann, *Theology of Hope*, 21.
16. Moltmann, *Theology of Hope*, 16.

Paul's statement that persevering in suffering leads to character, which leads to hope, should be seen not so much as containing an implicit command as offering a description of what happens in the lives of believers when they are confronted with trials of various kinds. Believers, like all human beings, have the ability to persevere: the difference is that they do so on the basis of and strengthened by the knowledge of what God has done in Christ. As the believing community responds to suffering which it experiences on the journey, it grows in wisdom, with an increasing appreciation of the nature of what it means to follow Christ. In this way, believers become hopeful people, increasingly able to exercise the gift of hope that they have been given.

Second, as we have seen, when we detect an implicit command in this passage, there is an (equally implicit) assumption that we may fail to obey it. But what happens if we do? Surely, on these terms, all we can do is to pick ourselves up and return to the tenet of faith which we have temporarily lost sight of, and carry on . . . until the next time. However, from the perspective of character ethics, Christian life is understood in terms of journey and growth rather than as a static condition of repeated failure and restoration. Along with others on the journey, we learn from our mistakes, becoming more mature and wiser as we do so.

Third, by relying on character ethics we have a much broader and richer understanding of the nature of hope itself. To be able to hope at all is, in this view, to have a "distinctive excellence" both in our individual lives and corporate church lives. But rather than being something for which we strive, or that we cultivate solely as a matter of obedience, hopefulness is a gift that God has already given us. It remains future oriented; its object is still the promise of the future revelation of God's glory to us and in us, and we are still part of the "now and not yet" with all the suffering and struggle that that entails. However, we are left far less to our own devices. As part of a community of faith, made up of fellow travelers who have also received this gift of hope, we are people who are playing their part in the narrative of Christ's continued work in the world. Looking forward to a time when God's glory will be seen, we are at the same time spurred on to serve others even in the midst of turmoil. We suffer, persevere, and hope together, encouraging each other and supporting each other in times of difficulty.

To be a believer, therefore, is to be a hopeful person whose behavior reflects the truth that the God who has a future good for us has become part one's being. Christian character differs from character understood without reference to God in Christ, because Christian character includes the theological virtue of hope and looks toward the *telos* of transformation. This is possible only because of what Christ has done and the fact that he has been raised from the dead. As for suffering, hope comes from the fact that we are sharing in Christ's sufferings and because God enables us to grow in a way in which we appreciate the gift of hope all the more. The statement that perseverance in suffering can bring about hope makes sense in so far as hope, given to us by God, enables us to grow and to become wiser, compassionate people. As we exercise this virtue, aided by the Holy Spirit, we are once again enabled to persevere. Hope is a matter of obedience, still, but it is a matter of exercising what we have already been given rather than mustering up the hope from somewhere within ourselves. We are also more able to understand the privilege of having that hope—which is a distinctive of those who are "in Christ." Our hopeful attitude of mind is a gift from God, which entails the hope that we will one day share in the glory of God, and a desire to bring something of that glory into the here and now.

PASTORAL IMPLICATIONS

So what does all this mean for people suffering from depression, who are no longer able to be hopeful? If we are inclined to see an implicit imperative in this passage, we are likely to see the struggles with faith and the sense of hopelessness that are associated with depression in terms of faulty, even disobedient, thinking that needs to be corrected. On this view, it is hardly surprising that those who suffer from depression and a loss of hope often feel that they are failing in their responsibility as believers, and feel an added sense of guilt, shame, and even failure. However, a character-ethics perspective enables us to take a different view of the loss of hope which is so common in depression. Believers who are suffering from depression have not had their gift of hope taken away from them, nor is their sense of hopelessness a result of willful disobedience or sin; it is rather a lessening, as a result of illness, of the ability to use the gift that they have been given.

Further, the foundationalist understanding of this passage led us to see the ability to hope as something which the individual believer needs to discover deep within themselves. A character-ethics interpretation, on the other hand, emphasizes that exercising the gift of hope is the responsibility of the community as a whole. Those who are suffering from depression remain part of a community whose distinctive excellence is hope—they need not feel that they struggle on in isolation. This, of course, is where pastoral care comes in. The pastoral care of those who feel hopeless is the responsibility of the community as a whole, and those who aspire to become agents of hope can do so only as part of the community of faith. Moreover, when we understand the Christian life in terms of a journey undertaken by people who are all prone to weakness, we are likely to have a more compassionate view of those who struggle along the way. We are all companions on the journey, each responsible for the support, encouragement, and care of our fellow travelers.

Lastly, the realization that hope is not intended merely as a psychological prop for individuals but as a stimulus to play our part in the transformation of the world is also important for our understanding of the nature of pastoral care. As companions on the journey of faith, caring for those who are in need, we can all become agents of hope. For, when we respond to the needs of those who are suffering, we are bringing something of the future hope into people's lives in the here and now.

CONCLUSION

In this chapter we have been considering Rom 5:3–4 through the lens of character ethics. In this view, everyone has the capacity to persevere when difficulties come, but for believers, persevering in suffering has special significance because it is part of the journey of faith in which we grow and mature in community. As we learn from experience, we become wiser and are able to grasp all the more what it means to be a part of the narrative of God's work, and to have been given the gift of hope.

We have also undertaken an investigation into the nature of this hope and seen that, while it is future-oriented, far from taking our attention away from real life in the here and now, it makes us all the more aware of the deficiencies of the present time and of the need to try to make things better. The understanding of hope as a theological virtue has meant that we see those who experience a sense of hopelessness as a result of depression not as people who are failing or even being disobedient, but as having a diminished ability to exercise the gift of hope. As far as pastoral care is concerned, then, the fact that we are "communities of character" who have been given a gift of hope means that we share the journey with others and support those who are struggling as best we can. We can be agents of hope in the "now and not yet" because we have the distinctive excellence of hopefulness.

Christian communities can be agents of hope in that, as we try to support those who are in difficulty, and as we work to alleviate suffering, we bring the eschatological hope into the present time.

There is, however, much more to say before we can consider our investigation of Rom 5:1–5 complete. For, we cannot have a full understanding of what it means to be a people of faith and hope without exploring the third theological virtue—love. Elsewhere in Paul's letters the ideas of faith, hope, and love are explicitly bound together. In Gal 5:5–6, in the course of his argument against those who wish to impose Jewish practices on Gentile believers, he writes: "For through the Spirit we eagerly await by faith the righteousness for which we hope. For in Christ Jesus neither circumcision nor uncircumcision has any value. The only thing that counts is faith expressing itself through love." In 1 Thess 1:2–3, he says that he gives thanks for the believers in Thessalonica as he remembers their "work of faith and labor of love and steadfastness of hope in our Lord Jesus Christ." And in 1 Cor 13 he famously says that of the three, the greatest is love (see also Col 1:4–5). While in these passages the close relationship of faith, hope, and love is evident, in Rom 5:1–5 this connection is not immediately obvious. In 5:1 Paul makes it clear that faith is the foundation of our hope. It is only because we have faith in the one who has raised Christ from the dead that we are in the position to receive this gift and assurance of hope in the first place. He also, however, says in 5:5 that hope does not disappoint, because the Holy Spirit pours the love of God into our hearts. In the next chapter we shall explore further the relationship between faith, hope, and love and the nature of love as a distinctive excellence in our communities. What does it mean to say that the love of God, which Paul says is poured into our hearts by the Holy Spirit, enables us to be agents of hope to those who may be feeling hopeless?

7

Love: Faith in Action

. . . and hope does not disappoint us, because God's love has been poured into our hearts through the Holy Spirit that has been given to us.

—*Rom 5:5*

There can be no true hope without love.

—*Augustine, Enchiridion 2.8*

INTRODUCTION

In our effort to read Rom 5:1–5 through the lens of character ethics, we have considered faith and hope as theological virtues. Both can be understood as gifts from God which are intended for the benefit of the church and beyond. Hope cannot be detached from faith, because our eschatological hope is grounded in and sustained by faith. It is because we know and trust the story of what God has done in the past and continues to do in the present through the work of the Holy Spirit that we too can be faithful and strain toward the future. Moreover, we have a part to play in the continuing story as we walk the journey of faith. The Christian community is, by its very nature, a community of faithful, hopeful people who share in Christ's sufferings together. But to be hopeful is much more than merely to cling to what we know, or to find a source of psychological and emotional comfort. It also spurs us on to alleviate the suffering we see around us, for the hope that we have means that we can see how things can and should be. If we are tempted to think that this is too difficult or even pointless, Paul is eager to reassure us that we have what we need to fulfil the task. The hope we have does not disappoint us; we may be confident because we have been given still another gift—the love of God. In this chapter, then, we need to explore what Paul means when he says that God's love has been poured into our hearts and how this relates to the ability to hope. From a character-ethics perspective, how does the gift of the love of God enable us to be agents of hope to those who feel hopeless?

AGAPĒ TOU THEOU—WHAT DOES IT MEAN?

We have seen that for Paul, our changed relationship with God gives believers a new understanding of the experience of suffering. The gift of faith enables us to persevere in times of trouble, and as our characters develop and mature, both morally and spiritually, so we are able to be hopeful people. In fact, he says, we can even rejoice in suffering, because through faith we come to understand it as having significance beyond ourselves: we are not only deepening our understanding of God's ways of working in the world but sharing in Christ's sufferings. The gift of hope enables us not only to glimpse how the story will conclude but to live compassionate lives in the light of that future hope.

But Paul does not leave it there. He has more to say about *how* this hope is sustained in the midst of difficulties and trials. Hope does not disappoint us, he says in verse 5, "because God's love has been poured into our hearts through the Holy Spirit that has been given to us."[1] The hope that believers have is not some vain delusion that will ultimately bring shame to the church.[2] This is no hoax; there will truly come a day when believers will "obtain the freedom of the glory of the children of God" (Rom 8:21).

1. The NRSV, NIV, and ESV translate *kataischunei* as present; however, there is discussion among commentators as to whether the verb should be accented as present or future. Moo, *Romans*, 304, for example, argues that since Paul's eye here is on future judgment, it should be considered as future. However, as Dunn notes, the eschatological hope has a present effect that is a distinguishing mark of the church (*Romans* 1–8, 252).

2. Kruse, *Paul's Letter to the Romans*, 231; Witherington, *Paul's Letter to the Romans*, 136.

Now, that is quite an assertion. The question is, How can we know that it is true? We can be certain, says Paul, because "God's love has been poured into our hearts through the Holy Spirit that has been given to us" (5:5). The use of the perfect passive indicative means that what has happened in the past continues to have significance in the present. God has given us this love and it remains active in our lives, evidence of the future hope in the here and now, made possible because of the prior gift of the Holy Spirit. But what does *hē agapē tou theou* consist of? What exactly is it that the Spirit has poured it into our hearts?

The majority of commentators understand the phrase as referring to God's love for us.[3] The main reason given for this view is that Paul goes on to say that "God proves his love for us in that while we still were sinners Christ died for us" (5:8). It is God's love, exemplified in Christ's sacrifice on the cross, of which the apostle speaks. As Susan Eastman says, Paul is speaking of "God's pre-emptive, undeserved self-giving on behalf of all humanity in the midst of its weakness, sinfulness, and even enmity towards God" (Rom 5:8–11).[4]

On this basis, then, we can understand Paul to be speaking of the love of God that is characterized by self-giving generosity, and that will be a constant in the lives of believers no matter what the circumstances (Rom 8:31–9). But what does this mean in the lives of those who receive it "poured into [their] hearts"? For many scholars, as we have already seen, it is a matter of subjective experience of God's love on the part of the individual. For Ernst Käsemann it is a deep certainty that God is for us. The phrase therefore denotes, "the solidarity which overcomes the opposition between creator and creature, which upholds the miracle of new existence and which at the same time continually brings awareness of it."[5]

Stephen Westerholm describes it as an emotional experience of great joy.[6] In other words, being in receipt of the "love of God" has to do with realizing how God feels about us.[7] By the same token, through the Holy Spirit, God enables believers to respond emotionally to the intellectual

3. See, for example, Gaventa, *Romans*, 145; Dunn, *Romans 1–8*, 253; Moo, *Romans*, 304; Kruse, *Paul's Letter to the Romans*, 321.

4. Eastman, "What Did Paul Think God Is Doing?," 210. Cf. Martin, "Reconciliation."

5. Käsemann, *Commentary on Romans*, 135.

6. Westerholm, *Understanding Paul*, 87–93.

7. See, for example, Dunn, *Jesus and the Spirit*, 201. Cf also Fee, *God's Empowering Presence*, 495–98.

apprehension of his love, and so "God's love forms the sure foundation of their hope."[8] Everything in life is now seen in the light of the knowledge and experience of God's love for us. On this view of the phrase "the love of God," the main effects of receiving God's love in our hearts are intellectual certainty, emotional reassurance, and a strength that enables us to endure. It is because of this that hope does not disappoint.

The view outlined above suggests that the love of God that is poured into our hearts is a one-way process, with the aim of reassuring and strengthening the believer. We know that hope will not disappoint because we have personal, experiential assurance of God's love for us. However, I am inclined to think that this is a limited understanding of the meaning of the phrase *agapē tou theou* here. There are two main reasons for this. First, for Paul, God's self-giving love in Christ has a purpose—the transformation of believers, who enter into new life and become more and more like Christ (see also Rom 6:1ff; Gal 2:20).[9] Second, it is clear from this and other letters of Paul that an ethic of love is central to his thinking and that this ethic is grounded in Jesus' own command to love God and neighbor.[10] It is difficult, therefore, to think that when Paul speaks of an outpouring of divine love he is thinking solely in terms of intellectual reassurance, emotional comfort, and a changed outlook on life. He must also be thinking of a transformation of believers' hearts so that they become people who love God and other people.

With this in mind it is instructive to note that it is also possible to understand the phrase *agapē tou theou* as an objective genitive that refers to the love of believers *for* God.[11] According to this interpretation, which was put forward by Augustine, Paul is saying that the Holy Spirit also pours love into the hearts of believers in order that they may be able to love God.[12] Martin Luther, in his *Lectures on Romans*, recognized the circular nature of the workings of the love of God. It is called God's love, he wrote, because "by it we love God alone."[13] Dietrich Bonhoeffer continued in this vein

8. Gundry-Volf, *Paul and Perseverance*, 51.

9. Spicq, *Agapē in the New Testament*, 36.

10. Söding, *Das Liebesgebot bei Paulus*; Furnish, *Love Command in the New Testament.*

11. Wallace, *Greek Grammar Beyond the Basics*, 121. See further, Wright, *Letter to the Romans*, 517.

12. Augustine, *Spirit and the Letter* 32.56, quoted in Bray, *Romans*, 130. For critique of Augustine's view, see Nygren, *Commentary on Romans*, 199.

13. Luther, *Lectures on Romans*, 162.

when, in a sermon on this passage written in 1938, he declared that the action of the Holy Spirit means that the "incomprehensible happens within" the believer, namely, "that he begins to love God for the sake of God and not for the sake of earthly goods or gifts, nor for the sake of peace, but truly and only for the sake of God."[14]

Exploiting the inherent ambiguity of the genitive phrase, then, we may now interpret Paul's words as follows: hope does not disappoint us because the Holy Spirit enables us to know and experience God's love for us, and also to be able to respond with love for God himself, "with the love of children for their Father" (Rom 8:15–16).[15] The first aspect of the transformation brought about by the outpouring of God's love is the enabling of human beings to move away from self-interest and self-absorption towards loving God because of who he is rather than what he can do for us.

The second aspect of this transformation is that the love that God pours into our hearts must turn our attention away from our own needs to those of others. Later in the Letter to the Romans, Paul insists that the community should be characterized by love: "Let love be genuine; hate what is evil, hold fast to what is good; love one another with mutual affection; outdo one another in showing honor" (12:9–10). Paul gives practical examples of how this love should express itself within the believing community (12:9–21): this diverse group of people must (among other things) extend hospitality to strangers, make sure that others' needs are met, share life experiences with one another ("weeping with those who weep"), desist from taking revenge, seek the good of the other, associate with the lowly, treat their enemies well, and seek peace and unity. It is a community which, though made up of people from very different religious and cultural backgrounds, both Jewish and Gentile, is to be marked by peace and mutual upbuilding (14:19 cf. Gal 5:13). This, then, is a community in which religious and social norms of the world are overturned.[16]

Moreover, in Rom 13:8–10, it becomes clear that this ethic of love is rooted in Jewish law (Lev 19:18) and the command given by Jesus himself (Matt 22:37–39; Mark 12:28–34). Paul writes,

14. Bonhoeffer, *Collected Sermons*, 192.

15. Spicq, *Agapē in the New Testament*, 46

16. Eastman, "What Did Paul Think God Is Doing?" does not take the view that *agapē tou theou* implies our love for God, but she does understand Paul as being confident that "recipients of such love will return love for God" (8:28) and one another (12:9; 13:8).

> Owe no one anything, except to love one another; for the one who loves another has fulfilled the law. The commandments, 'You shall not commit adultery; You shall not murder; You shall not steal; You shall not covet'; and any other commandment, are summed up in this word, 'Love your neighbor as yourself.' Love does no wrong to a neighbor; therefore, love is the fulfilling of the law.

When Paul speaks of the love of God being poured into our hearts, then, he seems to have in mind not only the apprehension of God's love for us but also the ability to love God himself in return. Furthermore, the outpouring of God's love into our hearts has a transforming effect on our behavior. It enables us to obey the command of Jesus to "love your neighbor as yourself" (Rom 15:9), thus enabling believers to look beyond their own needs and concerns to those of others. Bound together by a knowledge of divine love and by an ethic of love for God and neighbor, the community of faith has the strength to endure and be hopeful in times of difficulty.

LOVE ONE ANOTHER: A CHARACTER ETHICS-BASED APPROACH

There can be little doubt that Paul sees loving God and one another as the underlying ethical principle for life in the community of faith.[17] The parenesis in chapters 12–15 is rooted in the command to love one another.[18] Nevertheless, while the love command is important in Paul's thinking (see also Rom 13:8–9; Gal 5:13–14; 1 Thess 4:9), his understanding of the nature of *agapē* love in the Christian life should not be limited to command and obedience. The reason for this is that thinking of *agapē* only in terms of response to a command does not do justice to the idea of transformation in believers' lives which God's love brings about. True, the outpouring of God's love transforms our wills and so enables us to obey the love command. However, an emphasis on obedient action runs the risk of reducing *agapē* love to a matter of duty. As we shall see in a later chapter, it is quite possible for us to become so taken up with obeying the commandment that our motivation changes from a desire to serve God and others to wanting to ensure that we are "doing the right thing." In other words, a preoccupation with obedience to the love command can become a self-serving matter, wholly at odds with the nature of *agapē* love itself.

17. Stauffer, "*agapaō* . . . ," 51.

18. Konradt, "Love Command." On the Jewish roots of the New Testament love command, see Wischmeyer *Love as Agape*, 19–27.

An understanding informed by character ethics helps us to avoid these difficulties. Without downplaying the importance of the love command for Paul, we can suggest that certain emphases of character ethics help us further to understand the nature of the transformation that takes place in believers so that they become people whose distinctive excellence is *agapē* love. First, when love is understood as a virtue, it becomes easier to think about how our characters become transformed—in other words, how we mature and become people who are able to love God and others. Gradually, we change from being inward looking self-interested individuals to being concerned for the well-being of others, the community, and humanity as a whole. Of course, in order for this to take place we have to play our part and exercise the gift of love that we have been given—which will, of course, include consciously obeying the command to love. The crucial difference is that we know that this is not something that we must find in our own strength, nor is it merely a desire to do the right thing. Rather, we are given what we need to grow and mature into the loving people God wants us to be.

The second aspect of character ethics that helps us here is its focus on narrative. As we have seen, character ethics suggests that the way to learn how to be virtuous is to listen to the stories of our communities, for it is there that cumulative and collective wisdom is to be found. In particular, Christians learn how to be loving people by looking at the story of God's work in Christ. As Michael Gorman notes, for Paul the supreme example of *agapē* is to be found in the central story of Christ's self-sacrifice—the "master story" of love.[19] In the Letter to the Philippians, this story is found in poetic form in a hymn that speaks of the mindset of Christ,

> who, though he was in the form of God,
> did not regard equality with God
> as something to be exploited,
> but emptied himself,
> taking the form of a slave,
> being born in human likeness.
> And being found in human form,
> he humbled himself and became obedient to the point of death—
> even death on a cross. (Phil 2:5–11)

19. See Gorman *Cruciformity*, 168. See 155–77 for Gorman's detailed study of Paul's understanding of this story of love.

Christ's sacrifice, which brought about reconciliation between humanity and God, demonstrated exactly the kind of love that God has for his creation. It has at its heart a deep-seated willingness to let go of entitlement and to give up one's life for others. Gorman writes:

> Paul understands this love of Christ to have consisted of refusing to exploit status for selfish gain, freely renouncing such status, and preferring others over self by emptying himself in 'incarnation' (to use a later theological term) and by humbling himself in death. Although the hymn does not make these things explicit in itself, Paul's use of it does, and his use makes it clear that he sees the hymn's narrative as both a story of Christ's love, especially in his crucifixion, and a paradigmatic story about love to be followed by those in Christ.[20]

The narrative of Christ's love, then, gives us a far deeper understanding of the nature of *agapē* love. This is much more than a disposition to do what is required (however much this may be a gift from God); it is a radical transformation of attitude and thinking. It is a concern for others, certainly, but it is marked by humility and a willingness to forgo our cherished rights and privileges, real or imagined, and to act in the best interests of others rather than to please ourselves. We cannot stop there, however. The story of Christ's work in the world continues, and believers are called to participate in it. Christians, therefore, are called to love others self-sacrificially in the way that Christ himself did. However, this love can only be enabled by the Holy Spirit, who empowers us to become the people the adopted children of God ought to be (Rom 8:12–17), helping us in our weakness, and praying for us (8:26).[21] It is the gift of God's love that enables us to "be transformed by the renewing of [our] minds" (Rom 12:1–2), for we do not have the capacity to effect such change in ourselves. This is a true transformation of our inner lives from egoistic self-interest to care and concern for the building up of others.

This brings us to the third aspect of character ethics which helps us to understand how God's gift of love sustains hope—that of community. The emphasis on knowledge and experience that we have observed in the work of commentators could, for example, suggest that the love of God is given to provide emotional comfort and reassurance to individual believers. While there is an element of truth in this, the virtue of love is given not primarily

20. Gorman, *Cruciformity*, 168–69.

21. Rabens, *Holy Spirit and Ethics in Paul*, 209–37.

for individuals but for the community as a whole, and indeed for those beyond it. Self-denying *agapē* love is to be a "distinctive excellence" not only of individual believers but of our communities, which are to be remarkable in their difference from the rest of the world. These communities are made up of people who are willing to exercise the gift of love for the sake of the community as a whole and indeed for the sake of the world. The pervading pattern of power-seeking and selfish behavior that characterizes the world is challenged and undermined by sacrificial service, which does not seek its own glorification. Such love is not of an overtly heroic nature but is made up of "wholly inconspicuous acts," to use Joseph Pieper's phrase, in which the interests of others take priority over our own.[22] Among the believers in Rome, Paul envisages this love as manifesting itself in caring for one another (Rom 12:10) but also in the willingness to accept cultural differences, and in being willing to forgo one's own preferences and practices for the sake of the community as a whole.[23] More than that, Paul insists that vengeance has no place in the life of the community and instructs that believers should "if it is possible, so far as it depends on you, live peaceably with all" (12:17–21). *Agapē* extends beyond the boundaries of the community, which is called to love "particularly one's enemies, and to love without regard to the cost to oneself."[24]

Of course, our understanding of and ability to love is compromised by our human selfishness and clouded vision: we see, as Paul puts it in 1 Corinthians, "through a glass, darkly."[25] All our human attempts to love each other will be mixed up with our own desires, needs, and motivations, and so our efforts to love will be imperfect and flawed.[26] We will never fully be able to imitate Christ's kenotic, self-emptying love. Nevertheless, as we exercise the gift of *agapē* love in the community of faith, however imperfectly, we are together actively participating in the continuing story of Christ's work as we await the time of revelation as children of God (Rom 8:21). As we persevere in the suffering that this must necessarily entail, we mature in

22. Pieper, *Faith, Hope, Love*, 193.

23. Gorman, *Romans*, 266–80; see further Barclay, "Faith and Self-Detachment."

24. Murphy, "Agape and Non-Violence." See also, albeit from a slightly different angle, Hall, "Love." On the debate as to whether Paul extends the command to love to those outside the community, see Akiyama, *Love of Neighbour*, 149ff.

25. 1 Cor 13:12 KJV.

26. Note that I am not here endorsing the view of Anders Nygren, that *agapē* love must be divorced from our own human desire (eros) for what gives us pleasure. Rather, I take the view that God can use human desire and transform it for his own glorification. See Nygren, *Agape and Eros*. For critique of Nygren see Pieper, *Faith, Hope, Love*, 221–45.

character, learning from our mistakes. As we grow in wisdom, so we grow in our understanding of what love means. In other words, we become more Christlike and thus more able to show others the kind of love that God shows to us.[27]

When believers exercise this gift of *agapē* love, individually and in the community of faith, hope prevails. The ability to persevere and even "rejoice" in suffering (Rom 5:3 ESV) comes about through the collaborative work of the community of faithful, loving people, empowered by the Spirit. The eschatological hope of participating fully in God's love, which may seem so vague and distant, so divorced from our present experience, may be glimpsed now as believers put their own entitlements aside to care for each other as equals, and to reach out to others. When believers acknowledge their reliance on God, recognize their own weakness, and practice self-sacrificial love, they bring encouragement and hope to others. Hope is to be found in suffering, then, not merely by looking to the future, or by clinging to knowledge of what has happened in the past, although these are important, but by seeing the love of God working through people of faith. When believers exercise the gift of love, we enable the righteousness, peace, and joy that characterize the kingdom of God to be glimpsed in the here and now (Rom 14:17). Something of the future hope of God's justice and the revelation of his glory is brought into the present time.[28] In the expression of Christlike love we see something of how things will be when the full glory of God (who is love) is revealed.

THE LOVE OF GOD AND AGENTS OF HOPE

How then does this gift of the love of God enable pastoral carers to be agents of hope to people suffering from depression? From a foundationalist perspective, with its emphasis on obedient action, the most obvious answer is to say that our hope of one day sharing the glory of God is assured when we remind ourselves of the truth that God's love has been poured into our hearts by the Holy Spirit, experience that love emotionally, and obey the command to love God and neighbor. As far as pastoral care is concerned, it follows that those who are struggling to hope must be encouraged by being exhorted to do the same. They should remember Christ's sacrifice for

27. Hauerwas and Pinches, *Christians Among the Virtues*, 124. As Hauerwas and Pinches point out, however, we do not suffer in order that we will develop character. We learn rather how to become people of character because of and through our suffering.

28. See Moltmann, *Theology of Hope*.

them, recall the times when the experience of God's love was tangible, and do what they can to serve God and others. In practice, of course, pastoral care will also involve acts of service such as offering hospitality and helping to meet the needs of those who are in difficulty and unable to care for themselves.

However, while there is much to be said for such an understanding, not least in the fact that commands help us to overcome our own weakness, lack of good judgement and indeed laziness, we once again meet with problems when it comes to pastoral application for people suffering from depression. It is in the nature of severe depression that individuals tend to become self-absorbed, preoccupied with their distress. For many, the ability to apprehend God's love intellectually, to experience it emotionally, and to draw on the strength it affords is compromised, if not absent altogether. Any exhortation to do so as a matter of obedience is therefore likely only to exacerbate the sense of spiritual shame and failure which is so often a part of the depressed believer's thinking. Moreover, an inability, because of illness, to play an active role in the service of others may compound the problem.

A character-ethics perspective moves us away from the idea that spiritual difficulties of this sort represent failure or disobedience and toward viewing them as stemming from an inability (due to illness) to exercise the gifts that have been given.

To be sure, the person in the midst of depression may not be able to grasp that they cannot be separated from Christ's love (Rom 8:35–39), but the love of their community can help make the reality tangible in ways that may be understood only when illness recedes. To say that the community has the "distinctive excellence" of *agapē* love is to say that it is characterized by humility, selfless service to others, and a willingness to forgo one's own needs and preferences in the interests of others, including outsiders. It is made up of people who are gradually maturing into having the *phronēsis* or attitude of mind of Christ himself. Certainly, this entails following his example and obeying his command to love God and neighbor. However, we do so in the full knowledge that we cannot love in the way that Christ loves without the transformation brought about by the Spirit. Pastoral care has its basis in an acknowledged shared weakness and equality; those who are mentally "well" are not spiritually superior to those who are struggling. We are all of us companions on the same journey and we all suffer on the way. The role of the pastoral carer is to offer companionship and support for those who are struggling and provision for those who are in need.

As far as pastoral care is concerned, then, believers are agents of hope to those who feel hopeless when they love as Christ loves. However, the love that brings hope to those who feel hopeless is not motivated primarily by the need or desire to obey a command, nor is it conjured up by our own efforts. Christlike love can only be the result of a gift that enables us to love in the way that Christ loves. It is through the exercise of this gift that faith is expressed and hope—the insight that things can be different—stimulated and sustained.

CONCLUSION

How does the gift of the love of God enable believers to sustain hope? In short, we can say that the outpouring of the love of God into our hearts is the evidential, experiential, and transformative means by which we and others may, in the here and now, catch a glimpse of the time when we will share in his glory, unhindered by human weakness (Rom 8:17). Believers, who have had the love of God poured into their hearts (or as Anthony Thiselton puts it, into the "core of one's being") are being transformed into the likeness of Christ.[29] As they participate in the continuing story of Christ's work in the world, they are becoming people who are able to love God and neighbor in the way that Christ commands and exemplifies. In the midst of the suffering which is a necessary part of participation in Christ's story, they are increasingly able to love God and to serve others with humility and self-denying love. It is the exercise of the gift of *agapē* love that gives a glimpse in the here and now of the way things can be and will be in the future when the full glory of God is revealed.

The transforming love of God enables self-seeking individuals to become a community characterized by self-sacrifice, humility, compassion, and peace. Moreover, those who are unable to exercise their gifts of faith, hope, and love because of illness are not inferior to those who are "well." The chief role of pastoral care therefore is not to exhort and rebuke those who struggle but to provide humble companions who serve and support fellow travelers on the journey of faith, and as they do so, restore hope where it has been eroded or lost. We must now consider how this might work out in practice. In what ways can we be loving companions to those who are struggling to maintain hope because of depression? Answering this question will be our task in the next two chapters.

29. Thiselton, *Discovering Romans*, 126.

8

Romans 5:1–5 and Pastoral Care: A Case Study

SUGGESTION FROM A FRIEND
You wouldn't be so depressed
If you really believed in God
—*Jane Kenyon Having it out with Melancholy*

INTRODUCTION

In the preceding chapters I have offered two interpretations of Rom 5:1–5. The first, which adopted a foundationalist approach, suggested that in order to have hope in times of suffering we ought to remember what we know, persevere in order to become stronger in character, and hold on to the eschatological hope. Firm in the knowledge of what Christ has done, we will be able to live in the "now and not yet," knowing that one day our sufferings will come to an end. These verses can thus be seen as a source of encouragement in times of trouble but also as an instruction. When suffering comes believers should persevere, secure in the knowledge of God's love, and hold on to the eschatological hope.

Our second, more in-depth interpretation, which was influenced by character ethics and took account of certain recent developments in Pauline studies, came to rather different conclusions. Rather than taking "What ought I to do?" as the guiding question, we were concerned to find out "What kind of people does God want us to be?" We saw that from this standpoint, there is a move away from individualistic adherence to propositions and toward an emphasis on community and shared narrative, and a reconsideration of hope as a theological virtue (rather than merely a matter of obedience) along with faith and love. From this perspective, Rom 5:1–5 describes Christians as a faithful and loving people who are able to rejoice and persevere in suffering, grow in character, and be hopeful—less as a matter of individual obedient response, but rather as one of exercising, in community, the gifts they already have, enabled by the power of the Holy Spirit. In this chapter, I wish to explore further the practical implications of these two interpretations for the pastoral care of people suffering from severe depression. In order to do this, we will consider an imaginary case study of a pastoral carer, Emily, and her visit to John, who is a fellow church member.

CASE STUDY: A FOUNDATIONALIST HERMENEUTIC

John has been struggling with depression for several years now. He has been a Christian since he was a child, has been a regular church attender, and involved in church activities throughout his life. However, John has recently stopped coming to church. Despite having been prescribed antidepressants by his doctor, he is having difficulty sleeping and is preoccupied with thoughts of death and dying. He has started to doubt that he was ever a Christian and feels that God could not possibly love someone like him. He says that he can no longer see a future and that he feels hopeless.

Emily, who is a member of the church's pastoral care team, visits John and sits with him for a while, listening as he speaks of the darkness and hopelessness that he is feeling. As she listens, she becomes increasingly concerned for John's spiritual well-being. Opening her Bible at Rom 5:1–5, she reads these verses aloud. She urges him to remember and rejoice in what Jesus has done for him and to persevere through these tough times, holding on to the fact that one day, at the end-times, all will be well. She tells him that he should simply trust God and everything will be fine. Emily prays for John and leaves, confident that John will feel much better if he takes her advice.

John is suffering from a severe depression. This is having a major effect on his life, impacting him physically, psychologically, and socially. He is not sleeping well and is isolating himself from others. However, a spiritual dimension is adding to his distress. The change in his thinking brought about by the illness is not only affecting his ability to cope in everyday life; he is also finding that he is struggling with his faith. He is no longer able to have hope for the future. He does not doubt God's existence; what he doubts is God's love for him and his own integrity as a believer.

Emily is operating from a foundationalist perspective and believes that the Bible contains the information and instruction necessary to help John. Her knowledge of Scripture tells her that hope is a central feature of Christian faith, and she is naturally concerned when John tells her that he feels hopeless. She wants to help him, and believes that the Bible contains all that is necessary to enable her to do so. When she reads Scripture in her own devotional life, she always looks for encouragement and asks God to tell her what she ought to be doing. As she reads Rom 5:1–5, she feels that she is asking that question on John's behalf. Since the passage explicitly links faith, suffering, and hope, she believes that it provides the remedy for John's situation. So she tells John that in the midst of his suffering, he should hold on to what he believes, rejoice, and persevere. She believes that if he does these things, his faith will deepen (by which she means a deepening of certainty) and so he will be able to hold on to the future hope. Remembering God's love for him (even if he can't feel it) should also help him to maintain the hope which is at the center of his faith. Hope, then, is eschatological, propositional and a matter of obedient will.

Practical Implications of Emily's Approach

While Emily's good intentions are not in question, her hermeneutical standpoint and understanding of Scripture have some serious, problematic implications for her approach to John's care. First, her foundationalist hermeneutic means that she sees John's feeling of hopelessness and his loss of certainty in faith as problems that need to be fixed. They are, in her eyes, indicative of a faulty and weakened faith. Emily considers John's loss of hope to be a result of his having lost sight of the truth in some way, and Emily sees it as her pastoral responsibility to correct this. She feels she must remind him of what he knows, encourage him to hold on to the tenets of faith, exhort him to look forward to (hope for) the time when suffering will end, and urge him to remember God's love for him. Emily considers it her pastoral duty to read Rom 5:1–5 to him and explain how he can apply these verses in his life. Even though he may currently be unable to feel God's love for him, he can be encouraged to hold on to the principles of his faith by means of memory and intellect, and sheer strength of will. For Emily, pastoral care is a matter of applying a biblical passage to a situation and leaving the hearer to respond appropriately.

Second, Emily's understanding of the spiritual problems associated with John's depression carries with it some troubling implications for a Christian view of depression. In her view, John's sadness and struggles with belief and hope need to be remedied, for they ill befit someone who professes to be Christian. In other words, for Emily John's depression is somehow incompatible with his Christian faith. This is not an uncommon view. For example, in his book *Spiritual Depression*, D. Martyn Lloyd Jones writes, "A depressed Christian is a contradiction in terms, and he is a very poor recommendation for the gospel. Nothing is more important, therefore, than that we should be delivered from a condition which gives other people, looking at us, the impression that to be a Christian means to be unhappy, to be sad, to be morbid, and that the Christian is one who 'scorns delights and lives laborious days.'"[1]

According to Lloyd Jones, Christians should not be sad or unhappy. John's depression is not only a problem for him but for the church as a whole, for he is letting the side down. Others go even further than this and suggest that depression is to be attributed to sin. In John Piper's view, for example, a Christian who is suffering from depression should "probably be repenting and confessing the sin of gloomy faith."[2] Quoting 1 Thess 5:16, in which Paul tells his readers to "rejoice always," Piper declares that joy is part of our duty as Christians, and says that "failing to rejoice in God when we are commanded to rejoice is sin."[3] Piper focuses on the loss of joy rather than hope, but the principle is the same: the person who fails to rejoice is failing in Christian duty. On this view, if hope in the midst of suffering is a mark of Christian faith, failure to hope must therefore be sin. The underlying assumption here is that when people do not do what the Bible instructs, when they do not live up to its expectations, they must be deemed to be failing and sinful. Of course Christians do at times willfully disobey, and we must not lose sight of individual responsibility, for example, in matters of morality or in following Jesus' teachings. However, to assume that an

1. Lloyd-Jones, *Spiritual Depression*, 11.

2. Piper *When the Darkness Will Not Lift*, 49.

3. Piper, *When the Darkness Will Not Lift*, 50.

appeal to duty and obedience will be effective in a case of severe depression fails to take into account the complex nature of the illness. Turning back to our case study, at the very least Piper's view fails to grasp the fact that it is precisely *because* of his illness that John is experiencing spiritual struggle and a sense of hopelessness.

The loss of ability to maintain belief, to hope and feel the love of God is well described by Jan Dravecky.

> I was starting to experience moments of utter darkness, dark days when I would feel a black fog come over everything in my life. Nothing looked good; life had lost all joy. As I lay there in one of these black emotional fogs with strange thoughts floating around in my mind, I looked up at the sky through a crack in my bedroom curtains, and the sky did not seem real to me. I lifted my hands before my face, and I didn't even feel them. I couldn't feel God's presence, and I couldn't remember what it felt like to believe in him. Nor could I remember what joy felt like. I saw no light; I felt no hope; I had absolutely no strength left in myself.[4]

Dravecky powerfully describes the inability to hold on to previous certainties which can arise in depression. Her loss of joy and hope was not due to disobedience or lack of willpower; she was simply unable to think in the way she used to. Any attempt, therefore, to exhort her to have faith and hope was unlikely to be of help, for she would have been unable to do what was asked of her. The fact is, to tell someone whose spiritual struggles are the result of a severe depression that they should simply have faith could be as helpful as telling someone with a broken leg to go for a run around the block. Moreover, Piper's suggestion that the depressed Christian should confess gloomy faith could well be counterproductive. As Biebel and Koenig point out, "Depressed Christians are sometimes so painfully aware of their sins that this is all they can focus on."[5]

LAZY THEODICY

While Emily feels satisfied that she has dispensed the necessary spiritual medication, it is quite possible that John will hear only rebuke and criticism. Jane Kenyon's poem "Having It Out with Melancholy" provides a stark example of this. Kenyon quotes a comment made to her by one of

4. Dravecky and Neal, *Joy I'd Never Known*, 119–20.
5. Biebel and Koenig, *New Light on Depression*, 79.

her friends: "You wouldn't be so depressed if you really believed in God." The quote is presented as a single verse, and the lack of comment or reply underlines Kenyon's stunned reaction to her friend's remark. The implication is clear: Kenyon's faith is inadequate, inferior, sinful, and her spiritual struggles are her own fault. She can't really believe in God, or this wouldn't be happening to her. Her friend has adopted the position of spiritual judge and found her faith wanting.

Kenyon's friend's words are an example of what John Swinton calls "lazy theodicy," a simplistic form of thinking which blames psychological distress on sin or the demonic. "Lazy theodicy," Swinton writes,

> is lazy because it takes no time and makes no effort to explore the processes and experiences involved in the development of mental health challenges and the complexity of what is required for people to move toward healing and understanding. This way of thinking is not just lazy, it is also malignant, choosing to point the finger of "evil" at some of the most vulnerable people in our society rather than taking the time to work through the complexities of living with a mental health challenge.[6]

Lazy theodicy of this sort denigrates the experience of the person suffering from depression and, ultimately, serves only to boost the ego of the "carer" who is placing herself in the position of judge. It reduces pastoral care in instances of psychological distress to an emphasis on a moral "ought," which both fails to take into account the complexity of the situation and introduces a spiritual inequality which is unlikely to be helpful to someone suffering from severe depression, and which, as we have seen, may even compound their distress. It can lead to simplistic, inappropriate pastoral intervention that is at best ineffective and at worst highly dangerous.[7]

Lazy theodicy is also theologically erroneous, for it carries the implication that psychological suffering has no place in the believer's life, a view that is alien to Scripture. The experience of profound psychological suffering is frequently attested in the Psalms and the prophetic literature, and Jesus himself experiences extreme psychological anguish in the garden of Gethsemane. For Paul, the idea that problems and difficulties have been resolved for believers and that they should live "triumphant" lives is to be denounced with sarcasm (1 Cor 4:8). In fact, as we have already noted, he

6. Swinton, *Finding Jesus in the Storm*, 67.

7. See further Greider, *Much Madness Is Divinest Sense*, 189–98; Carlson, *Why Do Christians Shoot Their Wounded?*.

is at pains to point out that our inheritance as children of God is contingent on our suffering (Rom 8:17), which is a necessary part of the journey of faith.

Summary

I have suggested that Emily's hermeneutical assumption that Scripture represents a repository of information and instruction has certain unintended consequences when she applies Rom 5:1–5 in pastoral intervention. Her approach runs the risk of reducing pastoral care to an unequal power relationship in which the pastoral carer dispenses the information necessary to solve the problem, and in which the recipient's spiritual difficulties are attributed to fault and sin. Emily's view, I contend, fails to appreciate the nature of depression, and runs the risk not only of falling into the trap of dispensing "lazy theodicy" but also of compounding John's suffering by adding blame and guilt to his already heavy load. Further, according to Emily's foundationalist approach, once the information is given, it is up to John to take her advice or not, and if it does not work, the inference is that John has somehow failed or been disobedient. This could serve only to increase his sense of shame and may well prevent him from seeking pastoral help in the future.

A CHANGE OF MINDSET

Having identified some serious problems arising from a foundationalist interpretation of Rom 5:1–5 with regard to both our understanding of the nature of depression and the community's response to it, we must now ask what difference an interpretation informed by character ethics might make to the practice of pastoral care. At first sight, the answer to this question might be, "Not much." For if faith, hope, and love are gifts to be used, or distinctive characteristics to be developed, then we might be tempted to think that Emily simply needs to tell John to do just that—to use God's gifts, and to work on cultivating Christian character. This, however, would not only be to repeat the misunderstanding of the nature of depression which we have noted above, it would also be to fail to grasp the difference in mindset which a character-ethics approach brings about with regard to how Scripture and the Christian life are viewed and indeed, how pastoral care is carried out.

In the first place, Emily would have a quite different understanding of the Bible as a whole and of this passage in particular. Since the focus is on being rather than doing, and narrative rather than proposition, she would see the Bible less as a book of instruction (although this aspect is not lost) and more as the account of the narrative of God's work in the world and the source of knowledge and wisdom for believers as they participate in the continuing story. Accordingly, Paul's words in Rom 5:1–5 are understood not so much as an implied imperative as an account of why and how the Christian community is able to maintain and nurture hope in the midst of suffering. Christians have been given gifts of faith, hope, and love, which enable us to journey together and grow into wisdom and maturity. This is why we can rejoice when suffering comes, and persevere—for we know that God has given us all that we need.

This understanding will have a radical effect on Emily's view of John's predicament. As we have seen, from a character-ethics perspective, his struggles with faith are not seen as a failing in duty or spiritual flaw, but a temporary lessening of his ability, because of illness, to exercise the gifts that he has been given. She will not consider John's struggle with faith, sense of hopelessness, and inability to grasp the truth of God's love for him as failure or disobedience. Rather, Emily will see John as still on the inherently hopeful journey of faith. He may not be able to "believe that the journey is doable," and he may have lost sight of its *telos* altogether.[8] Nevertheless, he still is part of a hopeful community, the recipient of God's grace, still part of the story of God's work in history. From the perspective of character ethics, then, Emily's pastoral task is to accompany John through the difficult days of his journey, encouraging him and providing for his needs. However, she will know that this is not solely her responsibility, but the task of the whole community, whose collective wisdom and gifts may inform John's care.

AGAPĒ AND PASTORAL CARE

We must now turn to consider what this will mean in practice. How does an interpretation of Rom 5:1–5 informed by character ethics help Emily and the community as a whole to be agents of hope for John in his depression? In order to unpack this we will return to the idea of *agapē* as the means by which faith is strengthened and the future hope glimpsed in the present.[9]

8. Harrington and Keenan, *Paul and Virtue Ethics*, 98.

9. See Scheib, "Love as a Starting Point."

We have already seen that *agapē* for Paul is characterized by humility and self-giving. This humility expresses itself in voluntary servanthood associated with a willingness to set aside one's self-interests "in order to bring about the good of others."[10] So how can pastoral care reflect and be the expression of such an attitude of mind?

Firstly, Emily can care for John in many practical ways—visiting him, going shopping for him, inviting him out for coffee, accompanying him to appointments, and so on.[11] She can spend time with him, and listen if he wants to talk. She can learn about the nature of depression and be prepared to get medical help if John expresses suicidal ideas. It may be necessary for her to make sure that his environment is safe by doing basic housework for him or even removing sharp objects from the premises if she thinks that he is at risk of harming himself. She can learn about local resources and support groups for people with mental health challenges and their families. And, of course, she can read Scripture and pray with him.

Practical interventions such as these are vital, and can be life-saving. However, pastoral care cannot be reduced to practical tasks. It is, above all, Emily's understanding of the nature of *agapē* love that will be crucial in her ability to be an agent of hope in John's life. This will entail both concern for others and self-awareness. It is true, as psychologists Scioli and Biller say, that "the first step in imparting hope is to be available. When you are accessible to, reliably consistent with, and sensitive to, the needs of another person, your behavior reinforces the notion that goodness is present and the universe can be trusted. When you are absent, unreliable, or indifferent, it stymies the development of hope."[12]

Nevertheless, it is equally crucial to understand that the humility that is part and parcel of *agapē* means that Emily will learn to recognize her own limitations. It is not unusual for Christians to think that to be truly loving they must be willing to do everything and be available at all times: for example, it is common to hear sentiments such as "Jesus gave his all for me, and so I will give my all to others." This kind of thinking, however, is mistaken and potentially harmful. Joseph Pieper calls it "triumphal

10. Macaskill, *New Testament and Intellectual Humility*, 169.

11. On the general pastoral care of depression see further Moriarty, *Pastoral Care of Depression*; Meller and Albers, "Depression."; Gilbert, *Pastoral Care of Depression*; Carson, *Pastoral Care*, 1–21.

12. Scioli and Biller, *Hope in the Age of Anxiety*, 157.

misunderstanding," which "unrealistically and exaggeratedly portrays love as pure 'unselfishness' and, in so doing, makes the reality of love evaporate."[13]

This faulty understanding of *agapē* can cause love to "evaporate" in various ways. For example, if Emily does not look after herself, but focuses solely on John's needs, she may not only become exhausted and burned out herself, but she may neglect the needs of others, including those of her own family. She could also inadvertently cause John to become overdependent on her, stifling any self-determination that he may still have. It is crucial therefore to be aware of the need for healthy boundaries in our pastoral relationships, for our own well-being and for the well-being of those we are caring for.[14]

In fact, an important aspect of *agapē* is self-awareness. We need to be aware of when we are in danger of exhausting or neglecting ourselves. We also need to be aware that our motivations may not always be pure. It is possible, for instance, that an action or posture we think is unselfish could in fact be serving our own needs rather than those of others: a codependent need to avoid boredom, find a sense of self-worth, or gain the esteem of others.[15] As Ewan Kelly notes, in the field of pastoral and spiritual care, "there is a potential for us to immerse ourselves in the care and concern of others, seeking to gain our worth though affirmation from others and striving to achieve status and community recognition."[16]

Alternatively, it could be that we are unconsciously indulging a need to be in control of someone or some situation. Emily could, for example, be tempted constantly to check up on John, believing that this is an expression of love and care, when she is in reality trying to control his behavior. *Agapē*, however, is not controlling; it allows people freedom to take risks and make mistakes, and so to learn and grow.[17] In all these things, what starts out as good intentions may flip, without our being aware, into something less healthy. We need experience and wisdom to help us know when to protect and when to give freedom to someone we think may be at risk.[18]

Secondly, the humility that is part and parcel of *agapē* means that Emily will see the pastoral relationship in more egalitarian terms. A

13. Pieper, *Faith, Hope, Love*, 145.

14. Cloud and Townsend, *Boundaries*.

15. Beattie, *Co-Dependent No More*.

16. Kelly, *Personhood and Presence*, 14.

17. Vanstone, *Love's Endeavour, Love's Expense*.

18. Oord, *Nature of Love*, 27.

foundationalist mindset, as we have seen, tends to promote the idea that the person helping is in some way superior to the one needing help. However, the insights of character ethics will encourage Emily to see John as a fellow traveler on the journey of faith. Aware of her own vulnerability and woundedness, she will see her pastoral task as accompanying him through this particularly difficult time in his journey.[19] It is to be hoped that she will meet John with an openness that encourages him to express himself, and that she will be willing to learn from him. As Grant Macaskill notes, self-emptying (kenotic) love has to do with setting aside a sense of entitlement we may have with regard to thinking that we are right or that others are wrong, or that we have the right to enforce our views on others.[20] This does not preclude giving appropriate advice where necessary, but it does mean having the humility to learn when to speak and when to keep silent.

Learning to resist the need to say "the right thing" can be difficult. Carers can feel helpless and powerless in the face of suffering and long to be able to do something to alleviate it. It is understandable that so many people feel that pastoral care has to do with finding the right words, or doing whatever is needed to solve the problem. Ewan Kelly sums it up well: "As humans, we all innately want to make things better for others and ourselves, we want to get rid of pain and regain control; our first inclination is to stick a band aid on any open wound. Experiencing another's pain and loss of control in the face of death, serious illness or loss confronts us with our own fears, anxieties and helplessness."[21]

In addition to the feelings of uselessness, it can be deeply unsettling, and even threatening, to hear people voice their spiritual struggles, as this can touch on our own deep-seated ambivalences and fears. The kenotic element of agapē includes, I believe, resisting the impulse to "stick a Band-Aid on any open wound," being willing to allow space and time for doubts and struggles to be expressed, without giving in to the temptation to see these as problems to be solved.

Furthermore, it can be hard for carers not to fall into the trap of thinking that what helps them spiritually will help others. For example, people who find great comfort and solace in church attendance can find it difficult to understand why some people with depression do not want to go to church. In his memoir, John Colwell notes that when he was ill, he

19. Nouwen, *Wounded Healer*; Means, "Mighty Prophet/Wounded Healer."

20. Macaskill, *New Testament and Intellectual Humility*, 169.

21. Kelly, *Personhood and Presence*, 32.

found the joyous singing in his charismatic congregation hard to tolerate.[22] It may seem the most natural thing in the world for us to think that going to church will be helpful for someone who is depressed—surely the music and worship will be uplifting and the words spoken comforting? In fact, it can be the opposite. In our case study, if John is in agreement, sharing private communion together might be more helpful than joining in public worship.

The third aspect of *agapē* has to do with allowing our individualistic tendencies to give way to a greater sense of community. John's pastoral care is not just Emily's responsibility, but the whole community's. Those who are more practically inclined will be able to help with everyday tasks such as shopping and housework, or to invite him out for a meal.[23] Others will have a gift for patient, attentive listening. Communities need to be able to identify those with specific gifts and the time to offer for pastoral care. Not everyone will have the skills or time to stick with him, coping with the negativity and pessimism which so often accompany depression and which can be so wearing for those who seek to be "radical friends" to people with mental health challenges.[24] As Liz Carmichael notes, *agapē* "is not different from, or opposed to, friendship, but denotes the very love that makes true friendship possible."[25]

In these ways, the *agapē* shown by the community can be the agent of hope in John's life. The community's loving care and attention could be the way that he can begin to catch a glimpse of the future hope in the here and now. The practical evidence that he has not been abandoned, and that he is loved by God and accepted by others could be what he needs to begin, in William F. Lynch's words, to be able to "imagine what is not yet come to pass but still is possible."[26]

22. Colwell, Why *Have You Forsaken Me?*, 71.

23. On practical expressions of love for depressed people, see Biebel and Koenig, *New Light on Depression*, 227–55.

24. Swinton, *Resurrecting the Person*, 39. "The form of friendship here is radical in that it transcends the relational boundaries that are constructed by contemporary tendencies to associate with others on the basis of likeness, utility, or social exchange."

25. See further Carmichael, *Friendship*, 39.

26. Lynch, *Images of Hope*, vii.

CONCLUSION

In this chapter, I have suggested that Emily's foundationalist approach to the Bible has a profound effect not only on her understanding of Rom 5:1–5 but on her approach to pastoral care. Her view that the passage contains an implied imperative leads her to believe that it is her pastoral duty to fix John's sense of hopelessness by reminding him of what he knows and what he should be doing. I have also suggested that reading Rom 5:1–5 from the perspective of character ethics helps us to see the passage less as a source of instruction and more as a description of the kind of people self-understanding and her approach to the task of pastoral care. As a member of a community of faithful, hopeful, loving people, her role as pastoral carer is to accompany fellow travelers on the journey of faith, supporting and providing for the needs of those who are struggling. This care will be marked by self-giving love but also by a humility that recognizes her own limitations and the need to share the responsibility with others in the community.

A hermeneutic informed by character ethics enables us to have a much more compassionate and egalitarian view of pastoral care than a foundationalist hermeneutic allows. Pastoral carers become agents of hope to people with depression, not by telling them what they should know and do, but by accompanying them through the dark days of their journey. Certainly, this means attending to practical tasks, seeking professional help and offering encouragement, but it is a relationship of equals, carried out by the community of which John is a part. His sense of hopelessness is not seen as fault or failure, but his suffering is acknowledged and sensitive support offered. As Andrew Lester says, we hold on to the future of his story when he is unable to do so.[27] As Emily and the community as a whole accompany John on his journey, demonstrating God's love for him, he may be able to begin to sense God's love for him once more, and so to begin to regain his sense of hope. His sense of hopelessness is not seen as fault or failure, but his suffering is acknowledged and sensitive support offered. As Emily and the whole community accompany John on his journey, demonstrating God's love for him, he may be able to begin to sense God's love once more, and so begin to regain his sense of hope.

27. Lester, *Hope in Pastoral Care and Counselling.*

9

Mental Health, Wisdom, and Christian Communities

Hope cannot be built on a foundation that denies the reality of suffering. Likewise suffering is not to be "suffered" without hope.

—*J. Christiaan Beker*

INTRODUCTION

I have been suggesting that a hermeneutic informed by character ethics encourages us to see Paul's words in Rom 5:1–5 as wisdom, rather than instruction, for the journey of faith.[1] Suffering is a reality that must be faced, but the community of believers is given what it needs to help it persevere, and not only that, to grow and mature in the process. I have also maintained, influenced by Michael Gorman and others, that believers should understand themselves as participants in the continuing story of God's work in the world through Christ. This story is told in the whole canon of Scripture, and we can learn from the records of the ancient communities as they reflected on how to be the people of God in their particular situations. However, it is also the case that the church has never stopped learning what it means to be "communities of character" whose gifts of faith, hope, and

1. On "wisdom interpretation" of Scripture see Ford, *Christian Wisdom*, 52–89.

love enable them to be agents of hope in the world. In this chapter, I wish to draw on some of this wisdom, gained over centuries, that I believe to be particularly appropriate for the pastoral care of people suffering from depression. We will first briefly consider how liturgy, music, and art can be employed to help people who are struggling with depression to find ways of understanding and expressing, and perhaps even rediscovering their gifts of faith, hope, and love. We will then consider what can be learned from the traditions of acedia and the dark night—experiences of spiritual suffering that can mimic depression and are, in my opinion, sometimes mistaken for it. I shall suggest that an awareness of Christian tradition and wisdom of this sort can help our church communities to provide more nuanced and compassionate responses to emotional and spiritual distress than are often found in our contemporary medicalized world.

THE CHRISTIAN STORY, LITURGY, AND PASTORAL CARE

Liturgical practices enable us to reimagine, reenact, and grow in understanding as we participate in various aspects of the story of Christ's continuing work in the world. They can be profoundly healing for people who are going through difficult times. In the last chapter, I mentioned briefly that private communion can be of help to someone who feels unable to go to church. The intimacy of communion in the safety of home can be a source of encouragement to those who are not yet ready to venture out. For others, however, an invitation to a service or information about online services might be the catalyst for recovery. Barbara K. Sain writes, "The life of the church can foster hope when love breaks through isolation and the faith proclaimed by the community gives meaning to everyday life. Through the prayers and actions of the liturgy, the church commemorates the life, death, and resurrection of Christ, making the salvation that he accomplished for us present in our lives today. The community as a whole witnesses to the faithfulness of God's love, which is the basis for hope."[2]

Rejoining the life of the community, however tentatively, if met by sensitive (but not overwhelming) welcome, can revive a sense of belonging to something bigger than oneself. In particular, an invitation to communion is an encouragement to join in the centuries of Christian tradition in which

2. Sain, "One Body, One Spirit, One Hope," 212. See further Pembroke, *Pastoral Care in Worship.*

people have found nourishment and healing.[3] It is an invitation to participate in one of the means by which the continuing story of Christ's work in the world is witnessed and expressed. Pastors can also tailor smaller-scale services and liturgies for particular groups within their communities, such as a designated mental health service for sufferers and carers.[4]

Music too may speak to an individual where words do not. For William Styron, it was hearing Brahms's *Alto Rhapsody* that helped him begin his journey to recovery.[5] The expression of deep woundedness, pain, and lament in music can help us articulate our own pain, or can do so on our behalf. Music can also help foster a sense of the numinous. Familiar hymns or sacred music can be deeply comforting and help us to release emotion, thus bringing hope into the moment.[6] The same may be said for the visual arts as, for example, Henri Nouwen found as he gazed on Rembrandt's *The Return of the Prodigal Son*.[7] A knowledge of the interests of the person whom we are accompanying can be invaluable, for it can help us find a basis for sensitive, imaginative, and focused pastoral care.

ACEDIA

In addition to the treasure trove of liturgical and artistic expressions of spirituality that has built up over the centuries, there is much to learn from the wisdom the church has accrued with regard to spiritual distress and suffering. In the early church, hermit monks practicing extreme asceticism described a phenomenon they called acedia, which may be defined as "absence of care" or indifference. One of the earliest writers on the subject, Evagrius Pontus (345–399 CE), referred to it as the "noonday demon" (Ps 91:6) that "makes the sun appear sluggish and immobile, as if the day had fifty hours."[8] This demon afflicted the individual who was finding the daily routine of monastic life difficult: sufferers were beset with boredom, restlessness, hatred of their work and even of life itself. Writing around the same time, Cassian (365–435 CE), who wrote treatises for younger monastics,

3. Knight and Knight, *Disturbed in Mind and Spirit*, 30; Cf. Kelly, *Eschatology and Hope*, 181–200.

4. See Earey, *Worship That Cares*.

5. Styron, *Darkness Visible*, 66.

6. Clifton-Smith, *Performing Pastoral Care*.

7. Nouwen, *Return of the Prodigal Son*.

8. Evagrius Pontus, *Praktikos*, 12.

spoke of agitation and worry that made individuals want to escape their circumstances. This could have negative effects on the whole community, and the remedy was perseverance, prayer, and hard work.[9] Evagrius, Cassian, and others saw acedia as something that turns the person away from seeking what he or she knows is good—in other words, from seeking God. Centuries later, Thomas Aquinas considered the alleviation of acedia a matter of personal responsibility, helped by the grace of God.[10] Sufferers could learn to recognize it and even take steps to prevent it from becoming an insurmountable problem.[11]

These accounts of acedia describe a phenomenon in which individuals were afflicted with thoughts and feelings that could prevent them from seeking God, leading to dissatisfaction with and laziness in devotional activities. In other words, the temptation was to give up "participating in the life of God."[12] Today, as Eugene Petersen notes, in a society characterized by quick fixes and instant information, perseverance in faithful living can be difficult.[13] Committed Christians may become disillusioned with the daily routine of the life of faith, feeling that they are achieving nothing. They may fall into a spiritual torpor in which they wonder if there is any point in prayer, devotional reading, attending church and serving others. To put it another way, they become "resistant to the demands of love."[14]

Pastoral Care and Acedia

Because acedia is often accompanied by lowered mood and a sense of futility, it can be easy for pastoral carers to think about it in terms of mental illness and depression. However, there are important differences between acedia and depression. Although there may be some overlap, such as low mood and anxiety, in acedia the classic signs and symptoms of depression—sleep or appetite disturbance, poor concentration or fatigue, and a sense of worthlessness—are absent.[15] The restlessness is due to boredom and is not a symptom of disease. One crucial difference is that in depression the sufferer

9. Cassian, *Institutes*, book 10.
10. Thomas Aquinas, *Summa Theologica*, II-II.35.1.
11. Daly, "Before Depression."
12. Nault, *Noonday Devil*.
13. Petersen, *Long Obedience in the Same Direction*.
14. DeYoung, "Resistance to the Demands of Love."
15. LaMothe, "Analysis of Acedia."

longs to be rid of the spiritual struggle that can accompany low mood. In acedia, however, the person has no desire for change—the indifference is in some ways comfortable. It is simply too much effort to begin to care.[16]

The acedia tradition teaches that believers must endure the mundanities of life just like everyone else. It is easy to be distracted and deceived into thinking that the routine of daily devotions is futile. Boredom can masquerade as hopelessness. It is possible to allow emotions to overtake us, to become self-obsessed, and so to move away from God. It is at this point that acedia risks becoming sin, and we have a responsibility to do something about it. The ancients teach that the remedy is perseverance, prayer, and hard work, and looking after our physical needs. Thus, from a pastoral perspective, while rebuking the depressed person may be counterproductive, in cases of acedia, there is a place for challenging patterns of thinking and encouraging perseverance. For it is possible to learn what triggers the listlessness in the first place, how to work through it, and reap the spiritual benefits of resilience and self-knowledge.

Appropriate pastoral intervention can help prevent people from making poor decisions or avoiding responsibility, not just in their spiritual disciplines but in everyday life. Kathleen Norris wonders if "the restless boredom, frantic escapism, commitment phobia, and enervating despair that plagues us today is the ancient demon of acedia in modern dress."[17] She sees acedia as an affliction of our overbusy, consumerist societies, distracting us and preventing us from pursuing what is good in and for society, as well as for our personal lives. An understanding of the nature of acedia can help us to encourage people who are beginning to flag in their chosen calling, career, or marriage. In such circumstances, we can reassure people that times of boredom and distraction are normal, transient experiences, and encourage them not to be too much in thrall to their emotions.

JOHN OF THE CROSS AND THE DARK NIGHT

The second source of wisdom to be explored is the tradition of the "dark night." Although it is common to see a period of depression described as a dark-night experience, the two terms should not be confused. Depression, as currently understood, is a biopsychosocial phenomenon, while the dark night is entirely spiritual in origin. In order to understand the dark

16. Norris, *Acedia and Me*, 150.

17. Norris, *Acedia and Me*, 3.

night, we need to turn to John of the Cross, the Carmelite friar and priest who lived and worked in sixteenth-century Spain. John speaks of two dark nights, of the senses and of the spirit. The dark night of the senses refers to a time in the believer's life when all previous certainties are questioned. Everything he or she has relied on as spiritual "props" become suspect. The person no longer finds comfort or meaning in prayer or other spiritual practices. This dark night effectively moves the person on from discursive to contemplative prayer, and from relying on familiar practices to relying on God himself.[18] For John, this is an important aspect of spiritual maturation.

The second dark night, which occurs some years after the first, John calls the "dark night of the spirit." The distress and confusion of the dark night of the senses pales in comparison with the emotional pain and suffering of the dark night of the spirit. Everything one thought one understood about God is called into question. There is a sense of abandonment and rejection by God. "It seems," says John, "that God is against them and they are against God" (*DN* 2.5.5). There is spiritual emptiness, a sense of worthlessness and self-loathing, and of being unworthy of any blessing from God. According to John, this extreme suffering is a process of purgation—God is removing everything that is blocking the person's ability to be in union with him. The person must learn not to rely on his understanding of God and come to realize that there can be no such thing. On occasion, it may be relieved by a glimpse of the awareness of God's love (*DN* 2.7.4). However, it is important to understand that the pain is not inflicted by God himself, but is caused by the struggle that arises as the person tries to hold on to what is precious. In this darkness, there is hope, for that is where the purgation of the self takes place and individual is closest to God.

An experienced and sensitive spiritual director who knows that the dark night is part of some people's spiritual journey can accompany individuals through what can be a lengthy process. The problem from a pastoral perspective is, however, that the dark night of the spirit can mimic what we would today call a severe depression. The similarities are highlighted by the fact that John uses the same kind of language as some writers use to describe depression: he speaks, for example, of dark waters, of depths, of drowning. So how do we tell the difference?

18. John of the Cross, *Dark Night of the Soul* (*DN*) 1.8.3. See Kavanaugh and Rodriguez, *Collected Works of St John of the Cross*, 353–457. For an excellent introduction to John of the Cross see Matthews, *Impact of God*.

First, generally speaking, in depression the spiritual struggle comes as a result of the cognitive changes brought about by the illness.[19] The person's sense of worthlessness, sadness, and hopelessness lead to the belief that God has deserted them. In the dark night of the spirit, on the other hand, suffering comes about as a result of the spiritual struggles. The loss of certainties and the sense of abandonment can lead to a lowering of mood, which can become so severe as to be akin to a depression. In the dark night of the spirit, the person is still able to function in daily life. In severe depression on the other hand, this is less likely.

Second, in the dark night of the spirit, the person still longs for God and retains a desire to serve God, although everything, including his or her own psyche, seems to be rendering it impossible to do so (*DN* 1.9.3). In other words, hope remains. In depression, however, the desire (or perhaps the sense of being able) to serve God may be diminished as the person becomes less able to see beyond their own suffering and perceived spiritual failure.

Third, this dark night does not happen to new believers but only to those who have been on a genuine spiritual journey for many years. The person's preoccupation is with loss—loss of the spiritual experiences on which they have relied for so long and of the understanding of God they have built up over the years. In addition, there may even be a loss of the sense of self as all that is comforting is taken away.

Fourth, as Denys Turner emphasizes, we can distinguish the two by looking at their outcomes.[20] The dark night of the spirit can last for several years and will bring about spiritual transformation—a stripping of the ego and its pretensions—which results in an unsullied desire for God himself rather than what he can do for us.[21] When depression ends, however, the person returns to the previous way of being, albeit bruised from the experience and fearful of its return.

The Dark Night and Pastoral Care

How can we care for people who are having a dark-night experience? In the case study, Emily was sure that John's sense of hopelessness and loss

19. On the differences between the dark night and depression, see Bellini, *Cerulean Soul*, 137–43. Culligan, "Dark Night and Depression."

20. Turner, *Darkness of God*, 226–51.

21. Turner, *Darkness of God*, 236.

of certainty was incompatible with Christian faith. The dark-night tradition, however, teaches us that the need for certainty can be a hindrance to spiritual growth. The dark night is an ongoing spiritual process in which we are "liberated from attachments and compulsions and empowered to live and love more freely."[22] Perceptive listening is required in order to discern whether the problem is spiritual or medical. This may take some time, not least because the two can overlap. Sensitive questioning as to the person's preoccupations is important. Gerald May suggests that spiritual companions should help people to reflect on "what their deepest inclinations are."[23] In a dark-night experience, the desire is to be closer to God and deepened in faith, hope, and love. In depression, on the other hand, the person's desire is to be free of the emotional pain.[24]

Pastoral carers can make practical suggestions to those living through dark-night experiences. People who are going through the dark night of the senses can be encouraged to explore spiritual traditions other than their own. For example, resources from the Renovaré movement may help some to explore spirituality, while others may benefit from an introduction to the Ignatian tradition.[25] Exploring new Christian disciplines can open the way to a spirituality which is not hidebound by local, insular church life. In the case of the dark night of the spirit, pastoral carers can refer the individual to a spiritual director who has an understanding of the Carmelite tradition and the writings of John of the Cross. Whether those seeking help are experiencing the dark night of the senses or the dark night of the spirit, it is important for carers to reassure that the experience is a part of spiritual growth, and not to condemn or shame those under our care.[26]

While it is helpful to distinguish between the dark night and depression, we need to be careful not to be too rigid in our thinking. It is possible for people to have depression and a dark night experience at the same time.[27] The suffering caused by the dark night can tip over into a depression. Pastoral carers should therefore listen carefully and resist the temptation to

22. May, *Dark Night*, 4–5; See further Carson, "Sheer Grace."

23. May, *Dark Night*, 171.

24. May, *Dark Night*, 190–94.

25. From the Renovaré stable see, for example, Willard, *Spirit of the Disciplines*. On Ignatian spirituality see Lonsdale, *Eyes to See, Ears to Hear*.

26. On the place of dark-night experiences as part of spiritual growth and maturity see Groeschel, *Spiritual Passages*.

27. Scrutton, *Christianity and Depression*, 114–31; Bellini, *Cerulean Soul*, 137–39; May, *Dark Night* 156. But cf. Durà-Vilà *Sadness, Depression, and the Dark Night of the Soul*.

jump to conclusions. As we listen, however, we need also to be self-aware: those who are accustomed to working from a psychological or medical perspective may be more likely to think in terms of depression when they encounter spiritual distress, whereas spiritual directors may be more likely to think in terms of a dark night. Where there is any doubt at all, medical advice should, of course, be sought, preferably from a doctor who has some understanding of and sympathy with Christian spirituality.[28]

DISTINCTIVE WISDOM IN THE MODERN WORLD

A knowledge and understanding of the practical wisdom accrued over the centuries is invaluable in helping pastoral carers to discern the cause of spiritual distress associated with low mood and loss of hope. However, this wisdom can also help our communities to have a more nuanced understanding of mental health in general and depression in particular than is commonly found in our Western medicalized world. Following Aristotle, it is a commonly held view that the goal of human life should be to attain happy, fulfilled lives.[29] According to positive psychologist Martin Seligman, the aim is well-being or "flourishing."[30] However, for Christians the *telos* of the Christian community is quite different. The gospel, as Hauerwas and Pinches point out, confronts our presumptions about what will make us happy (or fulfilled). "Christianity," they write,

> "does not promise fulfilment but rather offers a way to live in the world truthfully and without illusion. That a people who follow a crucified God can presume life is finally about happiness seems odd at best. Christian convictions are more nearly true, not because they underwrite our assumptions about what constitutes human fulfilment, but because Christianity challenges our facile presumptions that God is primarily concerned about our happiness."[31]

28. See Williams, "Illness Narrative, Depression and Sainthood."

29. Aristotle, *Nichomachean Ethics.*

30. Martin Seligman is the most well-known proponent of "positive psychology," which promotes the idea of the virtues as important for the achievement of well-being or "flourishing." This is much more than happiness, as Aristotle argued, but consists of "positive emotion, engagement, meaning, positive relationships, and accomplishments (PERMA)." Seligman, *Flourish*, 16.

31. Hauerwas and Pinches, *Christians Among the Virtues*, 14. For further exploration of this idea of the *telos* of the church see Wilson, *Living Faithfully in a Fragmented World.*

The Christian community, then, is driven not by a wish to achieve happiness or well-being but by the desire to be disciples of Christ. We have seen that for Paul, the *telos* of Christian life is to be Christlike and in unity with God, and that faith, hope, and love (alongside the fruit of the Spirit) are given to us in order to help us on the journey toward this goal. Happiness or well-being may well be by-products, but how this is understood will be quite different from the individualistic success-oriented variety promoted by Seligman and others, and will have room within it for the pain, disappointments, and losses which are part of everyday human experience.[32]

Moreover, this understanding of our *telos* gives Christians a freedom from the burden of trying to conform to cultural expectations.[33] In this perspective, the individualism, consumerism, materialism, and quests for power that characterize our human endeavors to find fulfilment are shown to be shortsighted and limited versions of hope.[34] Of course, the development of this insight is a long process, but it is a pastoral responsibility sensitively and gently to teach and guide people in this alternative worldview. It is well documented that religion and faith are important factors in maintaining good mental health.[35] Furthermore, as committed disciples learn to see through the desires and values of society and, to some extent at least, are freed from its pressures, we will surely be less prone to the depression and anxieties which come are such a prominent feature of our modern world.

The Christian story gives us a different view of suffering in relation to hope from that of the outside world. In general terms, Western society has come to see suffering as something that must be avoided. There is a strong tendency to seek, where possible, the elimination of pain, including emotional pain.[36] Medicine, Stanley Hauerwas suggests, has as its goal keeping people alive: death must be avoided at all costs, for only thus can hope be maintained.[37] In the Christian story, however, suffering is not something to

32. See further Strawn, *Bible and the Pursuit of Happiness.*

33. Clements, *Faith*, 89–103.

34. Walls, "Wisdom of Hope," 259.

35. Koenig, *Is Religion Good for Your Health?*

36. This has led some to argue that psychiatry sees sadness as a disorder that must be treated: Horwitz and Wakefield, *Loss of Sadness*. Others go further and argue that the pharmaceutical industry has encouraged the pathologizing of sadness. See, for example, Healy, *Let Them Eat Prozac*. Healy's ideas were brought to a wider audience by Irving Kirsch, *Emperor's New Drugs*.

37. Hauerwas, *Naming the Silences*. The exception is palliative care, in which hope is to be found in bringing quality of life in the midst of suffering. See, for example, Buckley,

be banished, but is the catalyst of hope. If we try to exclude suffering from the Christian journey, we deprive ourselves of participating in a narrative bigger than ourselves, in which we are given "the grace to see our suffering as leading somewhere; as a part of a journey that stretches before us toward a destination that includes sharing in the glory of God."[38]

This is not to say, of course, that we should eschew what medicine has to offer. It does, however, mean that we are able to see that good can come out of suffering and that God is able to work through it.

The recognition that suffering has an important part to play in our Christian lives should help reduce stigma against mental health problems within our faith communities. We have seen the association of depression with sin or lack of faith in some Christians' minds. So too in some charismatic communities, mental distress is sometimes attributed to the demonic.[39] In these perspectives, Christians who suffer from depression are often considered to be inferior Christians whose faulty faith is potentially detrimental to the community as a whole. However, this is no different from the kind of stereotyping that labels people with mental health problems as "dangerous, unpredictable, incompetent, and unable to function in society."[40] This attitude marginalizes people within communities and contributes to feelings of rejection, failure and shame.[41] A recognition that emotional pain and distress are normal, indeed necessary, aspects of Christian experience, can help pastoral carers to walk alongside people with depression as equals and fellow travelers on the journey.

Finding Meaning in Depression?

Throughout this book we have been noting that for Paul, participating in Christ's suffering will lead us to our full inheritance. Suffering, therefore, is a catalyst of hope—which is why the apostle can say that it is an occasion for rejoicing. But does it make sense to say that for the individual concerned, the experience of severe depression (as distinct from acedia and dark-night

Palliative Care, 85–105.

38. Hauerwas and Pinches *Christians Among the Virtues*, 122.

39. See, for example, Trice and Bjorck, "Pentecostal Perspectives."

40. Yanos, *Written Off*, 4.

41. Bentall and Pilgrim, "Medicalization of Misery." See Swinton "Theology or Therapy?," 334.

experiences) can be a catalyst for hope? In other words, can meaning be found in severe depression? For those who take the view that depression has its origin in sin and that recovery is achievable solely through an act of obedience, the answer must be no: there can be no sense in which good can come from choosing to remain in sin.[42] Others come to a similar conclusion, though for different reasons—for instance, there can be nothing good in an experience that entails such profound suffering and can lead to suicide.

Some, however, are able to find meaning in their experience of depression. In his empirical study, John Swinton relates that some people see their depression as a kind of "crucible" in which previous assumptions and beliefs are melted into something new.[43] One respondent reported that depression enabled them to embark on a "fresh spiritual quest," which resulted in moving away from one expression of church to another, more helpful one. Similarly, in his book *Let Your Life Speak*, Parker Palmer writes, "Depression compelled me to find the river of life hidden beneath the ice."[44] He came to realize that his driven way of life was unhealthy and that change was needed. The experience of depression can also be transformative in the sense that it gives people a greater degree of empathy for and sensitivity to others.[45] Those who once felt hopeless may now themselves become agents of hope for others.

Some sufferers, then, do find meaning and positivity in their experience of severe depression.[46] Nevertheless, from a pastoral perspective, we need to exercise caution with regard to how we use this knowledge. We should not assume that the person we are caring for will find their experience of depression to be meaningful in this way, nor should we be critical of those who, for whatever reason, are unable to find hope.[47] Moreover, if any significance is to be discovered, it should be made by sufferers themselves—it cannot be imposed by others.[48] In fact, this realization will come only retrospectively, after recovery. As Matthew Ratcliffe notes, in the midst of the experience of depression, individuals can see only their pain: the sense of possibility for an ending to their suffering, let alone any good arising from

42. Scrutton, *Christianity and Depression*, 37–61.

43. Swinton, *Spirituality and Mental Health Care*, 92–134.

44. Palmer, *Let Your Life Speak*, 57.

45. See, for example Nouwen, *Wounded Healer*; Cf. Karp, *Speaking of Sadness*, 242–47.

46. For a discussion of the idea that depression might be potentially transformative see Scrutton, *Christianity and Depression*, 133–55.

47. Dana, "Suffering, Endurance, Character, Hope."

48. See Bellini, *Cerulean Soul*, 102.

it, is lost.[49] In Parker Palmer's case it took several years before he was able to see "how pivotal that passage had been on my pilgrimage toward selfhood and vocation."[50] Thus, we again see that an essential skill in pastoral care is to be able to discern when to speak and when to keep silent. Sometimes the loving (kenotic) thing to do is to refrain from sharing our theological insights into others' situations. It is quite appropriate to help someone who is experiencing acedia or the dark night to see that there is meaning and purpose to be found in these experiences. However, to say this to someone who is suffering from depression could be deeply insensitive and perceived as glib, insulting, and hurtful.[51]

CONCLUSION

In this chapter we have considered some aspects of Christian practical wisdom that can help us to take a more nuanced approach to the pastoral care of people who are experiencing low mood and a sense of hopelessness. Medical intervention may not always be necessary. Liturgy, music, and art can be valuable and powerful resources for helping people to find healing and hope. The traditions of acedia and the dark night teach us not always to think in terms of depression when people speak of low mood and spiritual struggle. A knowledge of these traditions can help pastoral carers to discern what is happening to a person and to respond appropriately. By the same token, an appreciation of the limits of our knowledge will urge us to seek medical help when the lines between clinical and spiritual phenomena are blurred or intertwined.

We have also seen that Christian wisdom can help us to nurture good mental health in our communities. As Christians become more Christlike, we become more aware of and thus more able to avoid the false hopes of individualism, materialism, and consumerism which are known to contribute to poor mental health. Further, the acceptance of emotional pain and spiritual struggle as a normal, necessary and potentially transformative part of Christian life can help us become communities in which the stigmatization of mental ill health in general and depression in particular is a thing of the past.

49. Ratcliffe, *Experiences of Depression*, 110–16.

50. Palmer, *Let Your Life Speak*, 56–57.

51. Scrutton, *Christianity and Depression*, 133–55; Swinton, *Raging with Compassion*, 9–29.

10

Scripture, Narrative, and Pastoral Care

"O Lord, in thee have I trusted—let me never be confounded."

—*Te Deum*

INTRODUCTION

In previous chapters we have seen that the hermeneutical approach taken when reading a biblical passage can have a direct effect on how it is applied in the pastoral care of people suffering from depression. Our first interpretation of Rom 5:1–5, which took a foundationalist approach, asked the question, "What ought I to do?" Our second interpretation, based on character ethics, asked, "What sort of people does God want us to be?" The first approach tended to see instruction in the text and concluded that hope in suffering is to be found as individuals actively, purposefully, and obediently holding on to what they have learned. The second drew our attention to the corporate responsibility of the faith community to exercise their gifts of faith hope, and love and so to bring hope into the lives of those who are in need of care. From this hermeneutical perspective, pastoral care is not so much a matter of solving problems and fixing faulty thinking and behavior as one of accompanying and supporting fellow travelers on the journey of faith.

In this chapter we will build on our findings from our study of Rom 5:1–5 and broaden the question to ask, "How might the Bible as a whole inform pastoral care of those living with mental health challenges in general?" In order to do this, we will begin by considering the work of two well-known foundationalist writers on pastoral counseling. We will inquire what the pastoral implications are for their views of Scripture. We will then explore further the pastoral implications of an approach to Scripture informed by character ethics, focusing in particular on the importance of narrative for understanding the biblical text and as a basis for the practice of pastoral care.

FOUNDATIONALISM AND THE USE OF THE BIBLE IN PASTORAL CARE AND COUNSELING

Jay Adams's Biblical Counseling

In our case study, Emily was sure that the Bible had the answer to John's problem and that it was her task to tell him that. This approach to the use of Scripture in pastoral care is found in the work of certain popular writers on pastoral counseling. Perhaps the most famous example is Jay Adams's "nouthetic counseling."[1] For Adams, 2 Tim 3:16 is seminal:

> All Scripture is breathed out by God and profitable for teaching, for reproof, for correction, and for training in righteousness, so that everyone who belongs to God may be competent, equipped for every good work.

He deduces from this that "there is no counselling situation for which the man of God is not adequately equipped by the Scriptures."[2] In Adams's view, there is no such thing as nonorganic mental illness, only mental distress that comes about as the result of sin. And for this, biblical principles and instruction provide the antidote.[3] Medicine and psychology can have

1. The term "nouthetics" derives from the Greek word for exhortation or admonishment (*noutheteō*): Adams, *Competent to Counsel*, 51.

2. Adams, *Christian Counselor's Manual*, 97.

3. See also Hunt, *Beyond Seduction*, 113. "Christians who turn from God and His word to psychotherapies for help with depression forsake 'the fountain of living waters' to drink from the polluted and unsatisfying and even harmful 'broken cisterns that can hold no water' (Jer 2:13)."

nothing to say on the matter.[4] All that is required is for counselees to hear what the Bible has to say about their behavior and to respond appropriately to its "admonitions"; then the mental disturbance will be alleviated. The role of the counselor, then, is to be directive, challenging counselees about their sinful thoughts and behavior.

It is clear that Adams's hermeneutic fully conforms to the foundationalist agenda of attaining "absolute, incontestable certainty regarding the truthfulness of [his] beliefs."[5] Scripture provides him with the information that he needs, both to diagnose the problems of those who come to him and to provide the solutions. Adams also approaches the text with the question, "What ought the counselee to be doing?" Moreover, his belief that he has the correct understanding of Scripture means that he becomes the expert with the knowledge required to address the problem.[6] His role as counselor is to challenge, rebuke, and instruct in order to bring about the necessary change in the counselee's behavior, and so in his or her mental state.

Adams's work has been influential in certain conservative strands of the church, and he has many followers today. There are, however, some consequences of his foundationalist hermeneutic that need to be noted.[7] First, his belief that the sole source of truth is Scripture itself, and that all mental health challenges (except those with organic causes) are due to sinful behavior leads him to a highly reductionist view of mental ill-health. There is no doubt that many people can and do become depressed if they indulge in what we might call sinful behavior; for example, people can be robbed of inner peace if they behave in ways that are at odds with their worldview, and the consequences of their actions can bring about great distress, for example in cases of family breakup due to adultery. However, to attribute all mental illness (including psychotic illnesses) to personal sin fails to understand the complexity of mental illness. As we have seen with

4. Adams did, however, accept that there was a place for medical opinion in cases of organic illness such as brain injury. On the debate as to how far, if at all, theology and psychology may be integrated see Entwistle, *Integrative Approaches to Psychology and Christianity*; McMinn and Phillips, *Care for the Soul*; Carter and Narramore, *Integration of Psychology and Theology*.

5. Grenz and Franke, *Beyond Foundationalism*, 23.

6. For similar views to Adams's, see MacArthur, *Counseling*; Law and Bowden, *Breakdowns Are Good for You*. See further Lambert, *Biblical Counseling Movement*.

7. For critique of Adams see Challis, *Word of Life*, 126–45; Biebel and Koenig, *New Light on Depression*, 157–60; Carter, "Adams' Theory of Nouthetic Counseling." Winter, "Jay Adams."

regard to depression, the causes may have biological, social, and psychological elements, and cannot be reduced simply to matters of behavior.

Second, Adams's idea that mental illness can be eliminated by changing one's behavior suggests that he thinks there is no room for mental health challenges in the church. It seems that if Christians are living obedient lives, they will not become mentally unwell. It follows that nonorganic mental illness and Christianity must be mutually exclusive. However, this view flies in the face of the attested experience of many believers past and present, some of whose voices we have heard in this book. These voices also have alerted us to the fact that Adams's approach has the potential to add to the suffering of those struggling with mental health challenges. While Adams insists that those whose sinful behavior he has confronted have responded to the exhortation with hope, we have heard the testimony of those for whom rebuke of this sort could easily have the opposite effect, serving only to add to the burden of guilt under which they are already laboring. Further, Adams's idea that Christians should not suffer from mental illness is, as Mark Meynell says in his thoughtful account of his own experience of depression, tantamount to prosperity gospel. Meynell writes, "So many of us have a sneaking presumption that if we have somehow done Jesus a favor by signing up to his team, he therefore owes us a stress-free time. So, if I go to church regularly, if I say my prayers and do good things for other people, then this is all to the good. I'm sure to be fine. I certainly won't get mentally ill. It's all a question of contractual obligations—on both sides."[8]

If we follow this line of thinking, Christians should all be healthy and successful (and, presumably, wealthy). However, such a view of mental illness is not only insulting to those in the church who struggle in this way, but it surely serves only to add to the stigma of mental illness, which so many people experience.

Third, Adams's rigidly foundationalist approach to biblical interpretation results, in my view, in an impoverished understanding of Scripture itself. It comes dangerously close to reducing Scripture to a book of principles and instructions. At the very least it underestimates and constricts the role the Bible can play in pastoral care. Little or no account is taken of the various genres of literature within the canon, or of the prevalence of narrative and wisdom over law and proposition. There is little acknowledgement of mystery or transcendence, biblical teaching being reduced to a matter of morality and right belief. Nor is there any recognition that there might

8. Meynell, *When Darkness Seems My Closest Friend*, 132–33.

be approaches to biblical interpretation other than Adams's own or that counselees might come from different traditions and cultural backgrounds. The counselee seems to be expected to accept Adams's interpretation of the Bible as the right one with no questions asked.

Larry Crabb

Not every writer on pastoral care and counselling who tends toward a foundationalist view of Scripture holds such extreme views with regard to mental illness and its treatment as Adams does. Others, for example, Larry Crabb, are prepared to give credence to secular psychology (he is himself a trained psychologist) and to allow that mental health challenges can have complex causes. Nevertheless, like Adams, Crabb sees the root cause of much mental distress as wrong patterns of living. The aim of counseling is to correct faulty thinking and in turn unhelpful behavior. He writes, "People pursue irresponsible ways of living as a means of defending against feelings of insignificance and insecurity. In most cases people have arrived at a wrong idea of what constitutes significance and security. And these false beliefs are at the root of their problems. Wrong patterns of living develop from wrong philosophies of thinking."[9]

In order to correct this, the counselor must help the individual develop "an inward character which conforms to the character (attitudes, beliefs, purposes) of Christ," and Crabb sees the Bible as providing everything that is needed for this task.[10] If, for example, the counselee recognizes and absorbs the truth that Christ died for us while we were still sinners (Rom 5:8), that is "at our worst, exposed for what we really are, no masks," then, according to Crabb, "the individual will be freed from a life of self-centered concern with whether or not his own needs are met, and he is able to move on to real self-actualization, confidently knowing (not necessarily always 'feeling') that his physical needs will be met according to God's purposes and that his personal needs are now and forever perfectly met."[11]

The main task of counseling, then, is to teach people to have right thinking about themselves in relation to God, and to help people replace

9. Crabb, *Effective Biblical Counseling*, 69. See also Crabb, *Basic Principles of Biblical Counseling*; cf. Pearce, *Cognitive Behavioral Therapy*.

10. Crabb, *Effective Biblical Counseling*, 29.

11. Crabb, *Effective Biblical Counseling*, 83–84.

wrong thinking. When this happens, behavior will change, and people will live healthier lifestyles.

A Critique of Crabb

Crabb's approach to counseling is gentler and deeper than Adams's nouthetics. Essentially a form of Christian cognitive behavioral therapy, it is gentler in that it prefers to encourage rather than rebuke, and deeper in that it seeks to help people with their thought patterns rather than focusing solely on behavior. Crabb does not support the view that all that is necessary to tackle mental illness is to identify sin and exhort change. He is well aware that this is simplistic and inadequate for the realities of real lives. Nevertheless, his foundationalist hermeneutic has certain problematic implications. His emphasis on teaching means that the counselor is again in a position of authority, for he or she is the expert who knows what is best for the person in distress, who knows what "right" thinking is. And while there is much more room for listening in Crabb's approach than in Adams's, he too is listening for fault—in this instance, faulty thinking. Ultimately Crabb, like Adams, considers the alleviation of mental distress to be a matter of obedience. For example, Crabb asserts that "Christian counseling is concerned with whether or not the client is responding obediently to whatever circumstance he is experiencing."[12] The onus is on the patient to do as Crabb advises, and it will be his or her fault if he or she fails to do so. However, not all mental illness may be attributed to personal sin and faulty thinking. Sometimes the faulty thinking is due to the illness and not the other way around.

Crabb's use of Scripture also tends to be simplistic and selective. Having decided that the difficulty most people bring to him is a lack of sense of significance and security he chooses Bible verses he sees as addressing that problem. He too neglects the rich variety of genres within the canon and is inclined to cherry-pick verses to be applied in particular situations, without taking into account the context of chosen passages, the arguments and purposes of the writers, or the bigger picture of the whole of Scripture. Although Crabb's mindset is more flexible that Adams's, he still offers a one-size-fits-all solution.

12. Crabb, *Effective Biblical Counseling*, 25.

PASTORAL IMPLICATIONS OF A FOUNDATIONALIST HERMENEUTIC

From our case study and our observation of Adams's and Crabb's work, we can see that a foundationalist hermeneutic has certain consequences, not only for how the Bible is used in pastoral care, but also for how pastoral care is understood. Firstly, the question, "What ought I to do?" leads the reader to look for instructions in the text. The need for certainty leads to a mindset in which there may be only one valid interpretation, with other views necessarily discounted. This has serious consequences for the use of the Bible in the pastoral encounter. The point of view of the counselee, if it is different from that of the pastoral counselor, must either be corrected or discounted. The carer becomes the expert, or at least the one with the knowledge necessary for change. We have seen in both Adams and Crabb an assumption of some kind of deficiency or fault on the part of the person in need. In Adams's case, the fault is to be found in the individual's behavior, while for Crabb, the problem is one of cognition. It becomes the carer's responsibility to pass on "biblical" information and instruction in order to correct the faulty behavior or thinking. Unfortunately, since the counselee cannot question the method or scrutinize the "medicine," it follows that if there is no improvement, he or she must be doing something wrong. The counselee must be guilty of faulty thinking at best, or at worst, sin. The counselor or carer can be tempted into thinking that he or she has done all that is required by "admonishing" and worse still, that the counselor is somehow superior to the counselee. A kind of spiritual pride and a judgmental attitude can creep in—traits which are incompatible with Jesus' teaching of love and mercy.

A second consequence of the foundationalist biblical interpretation is that the Bible is reduced to a reference book to be dipped into according to need. There is a tendency to atomize the text, looking for proof texts and instructions to apply to particular situations and to neglect the narrative which both rests at Scripture's heart and overarches it. The desire to know what we ought to do means, as we have seen, that we will likely look for implied imperatives in places where commands are not inherent in the text. For example, Adams lays great store on the book of Proverbs, seeing it less as a collection of culturally informed wisdom sayings and more as a set of imperatives disobeyed at our peril.

Thirdly, foundationalism, as the product of Western Enlightenment thinking, is individualistic by its very nature and tends to interpret the Bible in this way. This, along with the individualism inherent in counseling and psychotherapy, influences the use of the Bible in pastoral care.[13] However, the biblical writers themselves thought in communitarian terms. As Krister Stendahl showed in his study of Paul's letters, the apostle was not writing to individuals who were wrestling with questions of individual salvation, but with what it means to be a community of faith that is learning to live and work together.[14]

Lastly, the foundationalist hermeneutic that we have been examining has within it the risk, however unintended, of using the Bible in a coercive way. Consciously or unconsciously, the counsellor can impose his or her view on the counselee (who is likely to be in a vulnerable state) or use it to exercise power over them.[15] As we have seen, however, it is vital that pastoral carers be aware of their own motivations, values, and worldview, to have the humility to be aware that others may not share them, and to be willing and able to allow the expression of diverse views.

CHARACTER ETHICS AND THE USE OF THE BIBLE IN PASTORAL CARE

The foundationalist approach tends to result in an individualistic, proposition-based view of Scripture, in which the metanarrative of God's work in history is sidelined. Consequently, the Bible is often viewed as a reference book to be dipped into for relevant information for application in particular situations in individuals' lives. In pastoral practice, this tends to lead to proof-texting and formulaic responses. A hermeneutic informed by character ethics, on the other hand, enables a richer and more nuanced use of the Bible in pastoral care. Narrative, rather than proposition and principle, provides the basis of our lives and worldview. Christians live by the story found in Scripture and participate in God's work.[16] As Anthony Thiselton says, the biblical narratives inform and transform our lives, and "provide a resource by which readers can transcend the present," helping us to see

13. For a critique of individualism in pastoral care see McClure, *Moving Beyond Individualism*.

14. Stendahl, *Paul Among Jews and Gentiles*; Bailey, *Paul Through Mediterranean Eyes*.

15. See Brabham, "Pastoral Counseling and the Interpretation of Scripture"; Lynch, *Pastoral Care & Counseling*.

16. Hauerwas, *Community of Character*, 49.

another way of being and viewing the world.[17] Above all, we learn how to be human from the story of Jesus, who epitomizes a life characterized by faith, hope, and love.

The rise of interest in narrative in both biblical studies and pastoral theology makes it much easier for this view of Scripture to be integrated into the practice of pastoral care. Among biblical scholars, as we have noted, there has been an increased appreciation of the narrative that lies at the heart of the Christian faith and of the stories that make up much of the canon of Scripture.[18] In particular, Michael Gorman's understanding of the Pauline letters as written to communities that participate in the narrative of God's work in history has been important for this study. Our lives are woven into God's continuing story. Similarly, in pastoral theology much work has been done on narrative in pastoral care, in particular on the stories of people's lives. In his 1959 book, *The Living Human Document*, Charles V. Gerkin declared that "pastoral counselors are, more than anything else, listeners to and interpreters of stories."[19] We human beings need to know that we can tell our stories and that they will be heard and respected. As we tell our stories, we gain insight into our experiences. It is here that the pastoral listener has a role, for we also need to know how our stories fit into something that is larger than ourselves. This means understanding our lives as part of the grand narrative of God's work in history. Gerkin writes, "Practical theology becomes the task of maintaining the connections between the varied stories of life and the grounding story of the Christian community. Pastoral care becomes the community of faith's living expression of that grounding story."[20] Since Gerkin's influential work, the idea of narrative as a basis of pastoral care has become widespread.[21] Karen Scheib writes, "As a narrative practice, pastoral care attends to the inseparable interconnection between our own life stories, others' stories, the larger cultural stories, and God's story."[22] Scheib speaks in particular of pastoral care being grounded in the narrative of God's profound love for humanity. Collectively, and

17. Thiselton, *New Horizons in Hermeneutics*, 569.

18. See, for example, Wright, "Narrative Theology."

19. Gerkin, *Living Human Document*, 30.

20. Gerkin, *Introduction to Pastoral Care*, 111.

21. On pastoral care and counseling from a narrative perspective see Lester, *Hope in Pastoral Care*; Coyle, *Uncovering Spiritual Narratives*; Scheib, *Pastoral Care*; Doehring, *Practice of Pastoral Care*; Wimberly, *Using Scripture in Pastoral Counseling*.

22. Scheib, *Pastoral Care*, xi.

individually, we find meaning by means of the larger divine story of which our lives are part.[23] It follows that those who are involved in pastoral care must be rooted in the Judeo-Christian narrative that tells of God's love, above all in the story of Jesus of Nazareth. In this way pastoral carers can make sense of their own experience and begin to help others to understand theirs.

LISTENING WITHIN THE HABITUS OF SCRIPTURE

Pastoral encounters can be formal, as in the counseling sessions described by Adams and Crabb or in pastoral visitation such as Emily's encounter with John. They can also be as informal as a chance meeting in a coffee shop. Whatever the case, the first responsibility of the carer is to give space for listening. There is little doubt that counseling skills are invaluable in the pastoral care of people whose capacity for hope has been sabotaged for one reason or another.[24] Skilled listeners can enable and encourage people to tell their stories. As we do so, we enter the storyteller's world, beginning to see things from their point of view. Carrie Doehring speaks of "stepping respectfully and compassionately into another's narrative world."[25] Thus, whereas in pastoral counseling there is a relationship of expert and client, pastoral carers become "story companions" (to use Scheib's phrase) who listen for the presence of God in suffering, attend reverently to the story, and open themselves to learn from the other.[26] As fellow travelers on the journey, experiences and understandings can be shared and trust built up.

If the biblical story provides the reason for the pastoral encounter, it also provides the means to interpret it. The narrative of Scripture is our shared habitus, informing everything we do. As David Lyall says,

> The incarnation, God assuming our human nature, speaks of God *with us*; the crucifixion, God becoming vulnerable, speaks of God *for us*; the resurrection, death defeated, speaks of hope in the midst of despair, of life transcending death, of God *with us* and of the possibility of new beginnings. Whether or not these ideas are ever communicated verbally to the one being cared for, they

23. See, for example, Cole, *Be Not Anxious*.

24. See Lester, *Hope in Pastoral Care*.

25. Doehring, *Practice of Pastoral Care*, xvii.

26. Scheib, *Pastoral Care*.

> shape the world of the one who claims to care for the other. That being so, the context of pastoral care is one in which, no matter the extent of the distress revealed, there is a presumption of God's power to bring healing and renewal.[27]

The story of God's love for the world is thus a given in the pastoral encounter, at least on the part of the pastoral carer. It is because of this story that the pastoral carer can be an agent of hope. Thus, the use of the Scriptures is less one of applying them to the situation presenting itself and more one of relating the Christian story to what we are hearing and involved in.[28] Moreover, the story provides meaning with regard to suffering. The centrality of the cross to the story provides "a context in which human vulnerability and brokenness can be expressed, contained and transformed," and the resurrection gives hope for the future as we look forward to the time when the story will conclude and suffering will be ended.[29] As we have seen, for Paul, this meaning comes from participating in God's continued work in the world, of being coworkers with Christ as we journey toward the final times. With this in mind, from a pastoral perspective, the suffering caused by depression can be seen, not as something that must be dealt with as faulty spirituality, flawed thinking, or even sin, but as participating in Christ's own brokenness and suffering.

However, we have noted too that people in the midst of suffering may have serious doubts about the story or his or her place within it. Previous certainties may become eroded. It is here that the "presumption of God's power" on the part of the pastoral carer comes into play. Pastoral carers need to learn to trust the Spirit to work through them, without the need to control. They are freed from the need to find something to say, or of the need to be the expert in the situation. As the pastoral carer allows the Spirit freedom to work in the meeting, themes might arise from the person's story which can be related to the overarching biblical story or to particular scriptural stories.[30] Analogies might be drawn between the person's experience and those of biblical characters who struggled as they played their part in God's story, such as Joseph, Elijah, Jeremiah, or Job.[31] So too, the sto-

27. Lyall, *Integrity of Pastoral Care*, 102–3.

28. Lyall, *Integrity of Pastoral Care*, 28.

29. Lyall, *Integrity of Pastoral Care*, 101. Cf. Bauckham and Hart, *Hope Against Hope*, 41ff.

30. Oglesby, *Biblical Themes for Pastoral Care*.

31. See, for example, Stanford, *Grace for the Afflicted*.

ries contained within the gospels and the Acts of the Apostles show how communities of faith wrestled with how to be the people who were followers of Jesus Christ. Those cared for may identify with certain biblical characters and find their own resonances and lessons.[32] So too, Jesus' parables may provide images that can be picked up and explored, such as the lost coin or the lost sheep (Luke 15:8–14).

Scripture also provides us with the voices of those who have written about their struggles as they participate in the story. The honesty of the poems preserved in the Psalms has helped people find hope and courage throughout the centuries. The lament psalms give permission for complaint and cries of pain and anger in the midst of intolerable circumstances, leaving little room for lazy theology.[33] As Walter Brueggemann notes, the psalms of lament invite hope because they point to a reality outside ourselves and our human regimes.[34]

Reading Scripture together, without prescribed interpretation, allows the text to speak, allowing it to disclose as Ricoeur says, a world that transcends the immediate situation.[35] Understanding narrative as central to the use of the Bible in pastoral care in this way allows the person being cared for much more space to voice his or her own thoughts, questions, doubts, complaints, and insights. The carer's worldview and interpretation is not imposed, but may provide the background for discussion and exploration.

It will be evident that teaching remains central to the practice of pastoral care. However, while there may be a place for teaching within the pastoral encounter, in general it will be provided to the whole community by the theologically educated pastor or minister in preaching, formal teaching classes, and informal Bible study and discussion groups. The greater pastoral responsibility lies with the minister or pastor to ensure that the people of God know the story which they inhabit, that they can see their lives as expressions of the continuing story, and that they can begin to interpret their lives in its light. Thus will our faith communities learn the story of which we are a part, which gives meaning to our individual and corporate lives. The more we are immersed in the narrative of our community, the

32. See Van Beek, *Cross-Cultural Counseling*, 79–84

33. For the use of the Psalms in depression see Lewis, *Finding God*.

34. Brueggemann, *Spirituality of the Psalms*, xii; cf. Billman and Migliore *Rachel's Cry*. Cf. Swinton, *Raging with Compassion*, 5. See also McCarroll, *The End of Hope*, 97–116. On the use of the Old Testament in pastoral care see further Hopkins and Koppel, *Grounded in the Living Word*.

35. Ricoeur, "Biblical Hermeneutics." See further Thiselton, *New Horizons*, 351–57.

more its stories, themes and imagery will become available to us and inform our attitude and response as we listen to others.

CONCLUSION

How does a character-ethics hermeneutic help us in the use of Scripture in the pastoral care of people suffering from mental health challenges? It should be clear, I hope, that I am not objecting to the view that Scripture is central to the practice of pastoral care. Quite the contrary: as the repository of Christian wisdom Scripture is our primary resource. What I am worried about is a hermeneutic that so focuses on certainty and command that Scripture is reduced to an instruction manual, the Christian life to formulaic, unquestioning obedience, and pastoral care to a matter of instructing and correcting error. An emphasis on certainty and command, while appropriate in some circumstances, can have certain unintended consequences. Certainty may breed arrogance and insensitivity in the pastoral carer, and the focus on command may lead to an emphasis on instruction at the expense of listening and journeying alongside those who are in difficulty. The pastoral relationship can become an unequal one of expert and supplicant, or of superior and inferior Christians.

A character-ethics hermeneutic helps us to avoid or reduce these problems and risks. Its focus on narrative rather than instruction steers away from proof texting and nonnegotiable instruction. It opens up the whole body of Scripture with a freedom of interpretation in which mutual learning, accompanying, and support can take place. Placing ourselves within the metanarrative and stories of Scripture, then, helps us to absorb its message of God's love for his people and to understand ourselves better. I have been arguing that a narrative approach opens up many possibilities for the use of the Bible in pastoral care, possibilities which help us avoid the pitfalls we have already noted: inequality in the pastoral relationship, an over-emphasis on individualism, and (unintentional) coercion and disempowering of those under our care.

By understanding ourselves, both as individuals and communities, as participating in the narrative of God's love, and exploring the stories, characters, and imagery of Scripture together, we can find meaning in suffering, bring hope into people's lives, and—perhaps even more importantly—enable them to find hope for themselves once more. To a large extent, this approach is an exercise in humility: we recognize that we will never be able to "master" Scripture in all its complexity, but we can relish the adventure of exploration and discovery as we learn what manner of people God wants us to be.[36] Another way to put it is to say that our willingness to be open to Scripture, to be willing to forgo our own hard-won interpretations, and to allow the Holy Spirit to work in us and through us, without us having to be in control, is one aspect of *agapē* love. And as we have seen, it is love that brings hope into the world.

36. See Macaskill, *New Testament and Intellectual Humility*, chapter 8.

11

Conclusion

May the God of hope fill you with all joy and peace in believing, so that you may abound in hope by the power of the Holy Spirit.

—*Rom 15:13*

ROMANS 5:1–5, DEPRESSION, AND PASTORAL CARE

We began this book by noting the dearth of writing on the Bible and the pastoral care of people with mental health challenges In this contribution to the as yet nascent body of literature on the subject, our primary task has been to explore how Paul's words in Rom 5:1–5 might inform the pastoral care of people suffering from severe depression. We focused on depression because the sense of hopelessness that so many experience is the source of great suffering for many both within and outside the church. The sense of shame and spiritual failure that accompanies depression in the lives of so many believers makes sensitive pastoral care all the more important. We chose to focus on Rom 5:1–5 because here Paul explicitly links suffering and hope, saying that believers rejoice because perseverance in suffering brings about character, and this leads to hope. These words raise important questions for pastoral care. In what way can they be true for people suffering from depression? How can Paul's words inform the pastoral care of those who feel hopeless? To adopt Donald Capps's phrase, how can they help us to be "agents of hope" to those who are suffering from severe depression?

The next task was to find a hermeneutical approach which would enable the passage to speak into our contemporary situation. It was noted that much, if not most, use of the Bible in pastoral care literature tends to be rather superficial and simplistic, and seldom informed by biblical scholarship. It was suggested that this is partly due to the predominance of the historical-critical method in biblical studies and the method's tendency to widen the gap between the text and its contemporary application, and partly due to the prevalence of psychology in writing on pastoral care in the latter half of the twentieth century. It was also noted that there is a strong tendency among many writers on pastoral care to adopt a foundationalist hermeneutic (perhaps, in part, a reaction to the prevalence of psychology in the literature), which looks for certainty and focuses on proposition and command. That is to say, readers approach the text looking for information and instruction that may be applied in the pastoral setting in order to alleviate the suffering of individuals and help them overcome the difficulties they are facing, much in the way that a medical doctor might dispense medication. The problem with this approach is that Scripture tends to be reduced to a book of data and rules, and its use in pastoral care limited to proof-texting for use in giving instruction or emotional comfort. The recent rise of interest in character ethics, with its emphasis on narrative, community, wisdom, and the virtues offered us an alternative hermeneutical lens through which to view the biblical text. This approach, I suggested, would enable us to develop a more nuanced use of the Bible in writing on pastoral care.

Before exploring the text in depth, the next task, the purview of chapter 2, was to try to understand the nature of severe depression. We noted the criteria which inform the medical diagnosis of the disorder (for example, changes in sleep, appetite and thought patterns) and current approaches to treatment. However, it was also argued that, while it is important for pastoral carers to know what current medical and psychological thinking is with regard to depression and how to access it, it is even more valuable for carers to try to develop some understanding of the experience of depression. In other words, it is essential for those involved in pastoral care to be able to have some empathic grasp of what the person might be going through. Here we took note of the intense emotional pain and many losses which people suffering from depression report—of interest, of pleasure, of self-worth, of relationships, of work, and of hope. The additional spiritual suffering that such a "paralysis of hope"[1] (to use Sally Brampton's powerful phrase) entails for believers is a major pastoral concern. Loss of spiritual certainties and a sense of abandonment by God can add to the burden of shame and pain which many sufferers experience. Not only that—it is not uncommon for those who speak of such disorientation to be considered spiritually inferior to others in the community, especially by those who have never gone through such an experience themselves.

Given the loss of hope that is so much a part of the experience of depression, it seemed natural to turn in chapter 3 to Paul's words in which he expressly links suffering and hope and to ask how these verses can help those of us who are entrusted with the pastoral care of people suffering from severe depression. An initial exegesis of the passage suggested that for Paul, perseverance in suffering and dogged clinging to hope is the natural response to our knowledge of what God has done in the past and will do in the future—that is, God's actions through Jesus Christ, both in the past and at the end-times.

Adopting a foundationalist approach to the text, which asked the question, "What ought I to do?" led us to see an implied imperative within Paul's words: Christians ought to rejoice and persevere when suffering comes because of their knowledge of what God has done through Christ, the future hope that they have, and the experience of God's love in their lives. From a pastoral viewpoint, if someone is struggling to do this, it follows that it is the job of pastoral carers to exhort and encourage others to cling on to their faith, their knowledge of God's love, and the hope that one day God will be all in all. In this perspective, the onus is very much on the person who is going through difficult times to persevere and hold on in faith and hope as a matter of will. The problem is, however, that for people who are struggling with severe depression and have lost the ability to hope, the exhortation to trust and hope makes little or no sense. Not only that, but it could even add a sense of shame or guilt to an already heavy load.

Having noted these difficulties, we then explored in chapter 4 some implications of an interpretation of Rom 5:1–5 informed by character ethics. The question changed from "What ought I or you to do?" to "What kind of people does God want us to be?" Building on the initial exegesis, we would now focus in particular on faith, hope, and love as theological

1. Brampton, *Shoot the Damn Dog*, 3.

virtues, rather than as matters of will and obedience. In chapter 5, we reconsidered verses 1 and 2 of Rom 5 and explored the meaning of the Greek word *pistis* ("faith"). We concluded that the faith which forms the basis of hope is a God-given gift to the community which enables it to endure in times of difficulty. God gives us the grace to be believing, trusting, and faithful people. Certainly, as we persevere and exercise the gift of faith, we are able to see and understand more of God's faithfulness in the midst of trouble, discovering that he remains faithful even when we think he is not. So it is that we mature and grow in wisdom. But we need also to know how to live faithful lives, and from a character-ethics perspective this is learned from the story recorded in Scripture—in particular the story of Christ, who gives us the prime example of faithful living both in his own life and in his teaching. And as Michael Gorman notes, exercising the gift of faithfulness means that we participate in the continuing story and share in Christ's sufferings.[2] As we use this gift of faith, the community is transformed into a people who are able to be the disciples God wants us to be, able to care for and support those who are going through difficult times.

The understanding of faith as a theological virtue enabled us to move away from the idea that depressed believers' struggles with faith should be seen as disobedience and toward an understanding that due to illness, they are unable to exercise the gift that they have been given. In chapter 6, we reconsidered Rom 5:3–4 and explored what it means to persevere in suffering in order to be able to hope. Perseverance seen as a virtue is something for which we have the capacity (should we choose to use it) to learn and develop, and believers do this on the basis of the faith that they have as a theological virtue. Hope, too, is a God-given gift which enables the community to continue on the journey of faith. As believers persevere, they grow in wisdom and maturity, and as they do so, they are all the more able to exercise the gift of hope. One way of thinking about this is to say that they are able to see that there will be a time when things will be better—in other words, at the end-times, when according to Paul, believers will share in God's glory (Rom 8:17). We must not, however, think only of hope in terms of something which will come to pass in the future. As Jürgen Moltmann teaches, it is precisely because of our knowledge of how life will be and could be that believers must act to change things in the here and now.[3] The brokenness of the present should spur us on to work to

2. Gorman, *Cruciformity*.

3. Moltmann, *Theology of Hope*.

alleviate the suffering of others. In this way hope also plays its part in the transformation of the church into a compassionate community that serves the needs of others.

What this compassion entails in practice was explored in chapter 7 by looking in depth at 5:5, in which Paul says that hope does not disappoint because *God's agapē has been poured into our hearts through the Holy Spirit that has been given to us*. It was argued that the phrase "the love of God" could be understood both in the sense of God's love for us and in the sense of our love for God and others, and that the phrase should not be seen simply in terms of comfort and reassurance for individuals. Rather, God's gift of love enables us to respond in love for God himself and for others. It enables us to obey the commandment to love and, still more, to become people of whom it can truly be said that *agapē* love is a distinctive excellence. For believers, Jesus' self-emptying love for others is the paradigm to follow. As we exercise the gift of *agapē*, we are enabled to participate in the continuing story of Christ's work in the world. Pastoral care is a matter of accompanying those who are struggling on the journey of faith. When we live as Christ did, we enable the kingdom of God to be seen in the here and now. In the exercise of sacrificial love on the part of the community, based on faith and empowered by the Holy Spirit, something of the future hope is brought into the present.

If we ask Rom 5:1–5 to tell us what kind of people God wants his community of disciples to be, we can say that we are to be faithful, hopeful, and loving people. This, in turn, is the core and essence of the practice of pastoral care. However, we are not expected to do this out of our own strength but are given the ability to be so by means of the infused theological virtues of faith, hope, and love. The gift of faith gives us the basis and strength with which to persevere through suffering, and a hope which spurs us on as we look forward to the time when God full glory will be revealed. But "hope deferred makes the heart sick" (Prov 13:12), and we need some help in our present sufferings. This is provided by the gift of *agapē* love—God's love for us and the ability to respond to that love by fulfilling the commandment to love God and neighbor. Indeed, it is as we follow Christ's example of self-emptying love, aided by the Holy Spirit, that glimpses of the future hope may be seen in the community as it cares for those within its numbers and beyond.

Having established this as our revised interpretation of Rom 5:1–5, we were now in a position to answer the question, "How might these verses inform the pastoral care of those who feel unable to hope because of severe depression?" In each of the chapters dealing with Rom 5:1–5 we made some initial suggestions. The fact that faith, hope, and love are gifts from God and not merely matters of will carries the implication that the inability to be faithful, hopeful, and loving because of mental ill-health should not be considered as disobedience or spiritual weakness. This, in turn, means that the goal of pastoral care should not be primarily to fix a perceived spiritual problem but to support those who are struggling to maintain hope. Pastoral care becomes a matter of accompanying and supporting fellow travelers on the journey of faith, rather than of addressing and trying to fix perceived spiritual shortcomings. We are all equals on the journey of faith, and pastoral care is the concern of the community as a whole. We become agents of hope by exercising the gift of selfless *agapē* love enabled by the Spirit.

The next step was to explore how this might work out in practice. In order to do this, in chapter 8 a case study was presented in which some of the implications of a foundationalist approach were explored further and potential difficulties brought to light. We noted again that foundationalist thinking tends to promote a view of pastoral care as an unequal relationship in which it is the task of the "well" to sort out the problems of those who are "sick." In this case, Emily believed that John's struggles with faith and hope were problematic and could be fixed by reading the biblical passage. She saw it as her responsibility to remind John of what he needed to know and do. The question, "What ought I to do?" (and, by extension, "What ought the person for whom I am caring to do?") encouraged Emily to use the biblical text prescriptively to try to fix what she perceived as a spiritual problem. Further, her tendency to find an implicit instruction in the passage ran the risk of an understanding that those who are unable to obey that instruction are somehow second-class Christians who are letting the side down. Besides the potential for adding to John's already heavy burden, we noted too the risk of what John Swinton calls "lazy theodicy," which denigrates suffering, creates inequality between the sick and the well, and serves only to prop up the ego of the pastoral carer.

When we adopted the lens of character ethics, on the other hand, and asked the question, "What kind of people does God want us to be?" Scripture became less a book of doctrine and instruction and more a source of wisdom on which believers can draw as they participate in the continuing story of Christ's work in the world. In this perspective, in Rom 5:1–5 Paul is sure that the believing community will not be overwhelmed by suffering but will be able to see that hope can come because believers are faithful, hopeful, loving people who have been given what they need in order to endure when suffering comes, as it inevitably will. As participants in the continuing story of God's work in the world, they are enabled through the gift of faith to hold on to what they know, to trust in its continuing truth, and to be faithful, as Christ himself was faithful to God's purposes. The gift of hope enables believers to press on to the future in which God's purposes will be fully revealed, and they too will be revealed as the sons and daughters of God. The gift of *agapē* love enables them to love God and others.

In severe depression, however, the ability to exercise these gifts is, for many, diminished. It can be all but impossible to be faithful, to maintain hope, and to be able to reach out to others when one is in the midst of extreme emotional pain. In such a situation it is the role of pastoral carers to use their gifts of faith, hope, and love on behalf of those who are struggling to do so. Pastoral care is a community responsibility to accompany and support fellow travelers on the journey of faith who are going through difficult times. In particular, it is through the practice of *agapē* love that the community can be agents of hope for those who feel hopeless. This will, of course, include practical help and sensitive listening, but the nature of self-denying agapē means that any help we might offer will be tempered with humility and self-awareness with regard to our gifts, limitations, vulnerabilities, and motivations.

As the gift of *agapē* is exercised in the community, it may just be that those who feel hopeless can catch a glimpse of divine glory in the here and now, and so begin to regain a sense of how faith, hope, and love might play out in their own lives.

HERMENEUTICS, MENTAL HEALTH, AND PASTORAL CARE

The main part of this book has been concerned with how Paul's words in Rom 5:1–5 might inform the pastoral care of people suffering from severe depression. However, in the course of the study it has become clear that a move away from a foundationalist hermeneutic to one informed by character ethics has profound implications not only for our approach to the text itself but for our understanding of the nature of depression and the spiritual experience of those who suffer from it, for our understanding of pastoral care itself, and for our appreciation of the place of Scripture within its practice. In chapters 9 and 10, we went on to explore some of these broader implications of our study.

In chapter 9, we drew further on the ideas of narrative and wisdom, which are so central to character ethics. Recognizing that the Christian story continues even in the postbiblical age, we set out to learn from some of the wisdom which has accrued over the centuries and to apply it to the pastoral care of people with severe depression. We saw that liturgical practices, music, and art can help people suffering from depression to express their feelings and can be an aid to recovery. The main part of this chapter, however, was devoted to exploring two Christian traditions that can help us to have a more nuanced understanding of the relationship between low mood and spiritual experience. Firstly, the condition known from ancient times as acedia teaches that spiritual boredom and restlessness may produce low mood and imitate what we might today describe as depression. Acedia is a spiritual rather than a clinical concern, however, and is one instance in which exhortation to persevere in spiritual practices may indeed be appropriate—we may even be able to encourage someone to continue in their calling through the mundanities of everyday life. Secondly, we noted the Carmelite tradition of the "dark night," in which previous certainties are eroded, and observed that the distress caused by this experience can imitate and even tip over into depression. A knowledgeable and skillful pastoral carer can learn to distinguish between the two. Lastly, we saw that wisdom can help us to see that the Christian worldview is quite different from that of the modern world, whose *telos* is often perceived to be happiness. The Christian *telos*, on the other hand, is unity with God, transformation into Christlikeness. It was suggested that when Christians realize this crucial difference, they can be freed from many of the pressures of contemporary life and so be less prone to depression.

In chapter 10, we explored in greater depth how this approach might inform the use of the Bible in pastoral care. We first offered a critique of two popular and influential writers on pastoral counseling who approach the biblical text from a foundationalist perspective, Jay Adams and Larry Crabb. While there are important differences between the two writers, both see the alleviation of mental distress to be a matter of obedience to biblical precepts and principles. The pastoral counselor is the expert whose role is to impart this knowledge and correct faulty behavior or thinking. Not only is pastoral counselling reduced to the correction and exhortation of individuals by individuals, but the Bible is reduced to a reference book containing information and instruction to be dispensed as the counselor sees fit, with little or no room for questioning on the part of the sufferer. The risk of a coercive use of Scripture is not far away.

A hermeneutic informed by character ethics offers us a richer, more nuanced and compassionate understanding of the role of Scripture in pastoral care. The highlighting of community leads us away from an individualistic notion of the practice of pastoral care toward collaboration and the shared use of different gifts within congregations and communities. The emphasis on character, wisdom and the virtues helps us to focus on becoming the kind of people God wants us to be rather than on rules and instruction. The prominence of narrative helps us to have a broader, less atomizing view of Scripture. As Karen Scheib says, pastoral care is rooted in the story of God's love and gives space for others to tell their stories. Pastoral carers give space for others to tell their stories, becoming "story companions," who listen and seek to understand the experience of others in the light of the story of God's love for the world.[4]

Although I have here advocated the use of a hermeneutic based on character ethics, it is important to note that I am not suggesting that a foundationalist hermeneutic will always result in the kind of pastoral intervention we have outlined in this book—that it will always preclude sensitive listening, community-based practical support of individuals and their families, or indeed patient accompaniment through the experience. Many people who operate from a foundationalist perspective can and do exercise compassion in pastoral care, and do so with humility and wisdom. Nevertheless, I do believe that a foundationalist outlook carries a greater risk of a reductionism which, in the case of severe depression, may well add to the suffering of those being cared for.[5] I am suggesting, therefore, that the foundationalist hermeneutic, preoccupied as it is with data and certainty, carries the greater risk of a theologically simplistic mindset that attributes spiritual struggle to sin or fault, and so contributes to the marginalizing of people suffering from mental health challenges within the church.

The need for certainty which is at the heart of the foundationalist mindset is, I believe, ultimately incompatible with the humility of agapē love, which is willing to serve others without clinging to our most cherished ideas. At the very least, I suggest, the character ethics-based hermeneutic explored in this book will help us avoid the kind of approach to pastoral

4. Scheib, *Pastoral Care*, 61.

5. On spiritual suffering see Bartel, "What Is Spiritual?"

care which has caused alienation and compounded suffering of the sort we saw in the accounts of Christians in chapter 2. I hope, too, that the focus on pastoral care as accompaniment on the journey of faith on the part of the whole community will reduce the stigma against mental health challenges—stigma that so many experience and that should have no place in the church today.

Throughout the book, it has been my desire to integrate pastoral theology and biblical studies in a way that does justice to both disciplines. I have wanted in particular to provide an exploration of Rom 5:1–5 that takes the insights of biblical scholarship seriously in order to bring out the depths and riches of Paul's words for pastoral care. It will be evident that the work has been borne out of frustration—frustration with works on pastoral theology that, as I argued in the introduction, tend to use the Bible in a simplistic and superficial way. We owe it to the Scriptures themselves to treat them with respect, to value their depths and riches, and to use the resources of scholarship to bring these riches to the service of pastoral theology. We owe it to the church to allow the biblical literature to inform our pastoral care in sensitive and nuanced ways that are respectful to both Scripture and the people in our care. It is my hope that the arguments and flaws of this book will contribute to further interdisciplinary discussion for the benefit of the church as a whole.

In the introduction we noted John Swinton's call for a mental health hermeneutic. Swinton's desire, like mine, is for compassionate use of the Bible in the pastoral care of people with mental health challenges. Nevertheless, I doubt if there can be a single mental health hermeneutic, or indeed that there should be, not least because of the sheer variety of experience among those who are "in front of the text"—that is, because of the complexity of human nature and of mental health problems themselves. What I have offered here, by way of a test case, is a suggestion that character ethics provides us with a healthy, humble, and nuanced way of way of approaching both the Bible and pastoral care which can be transformational both for those of us who are involved in pastoral work and for those for whom we are caring.[6] I do not suggest that character ethics is the only hermeneutical lens for the task, but offer it as one approach among many which can contribute to this, I hope, growing field of research.

As we come to the end of our study, it seems fitting to return to the Epistle to the Romans, which has been so important for our understanding

6. Brown, preface, xii.

of the nature of Christian hope. When Paul wrote this letter, he was attempting to help a group of new believers to understand what it means to be disciples of Christ in a difficult, sometimes hostile environment. The letter is, in some respects, a pastoral intervention intended to encourage and support those who may have been at risk of losing sight of the hope that was at the center of their newfound faith. The group was marginalized in society, held to be subversive, and viewed with suspicion. Paul, as pastor, was concerned that they should be resilient and hopeful in the face of stigma and rejection. As he nears the conclusion of his long discourse to these vulnerable believers he makes the following prayer:

> May the God of hope fill you with all joy and peace in believing, so that you may abound in hope by the power of the Holy Spirit. (15:13)

The same prayer may be made for those who are suffering from depression today, who are at risk of misunderstanding and isolation within our churches, as well as for those who seek to support them through the times when hope seems impossible to maintain. May those who feel hopeless be nurtured through the gift of *agapē* love, cared for and supported by communities of faith who dare to hope on their behalf.

Bibliography

Abramson, Lyn Y., et al. "Hopelessness Depression: A Theory-Based Subtype of Depression." *Psychological Review* 96 (1989) 358–72.

Achtemeier, Paul J. *Romans*. IBC. Atlanta: John Knox, 1985.

Adams, Edward. *The Stars Will Fall from Heaven: Cosmic Catastrophe in the New Testament and Its World*. T. & T. Clark Library of Biblical Studies. LNTS 347. London: T. & T. Clark, 2007.

Adams, Jay E. *The Christian Counselor's Manual: The Practice of Nouthetic Counseling*. The Jay Adams Library. Grand Rapids: Zondervan, 1986.

———. *Competent to Counsel: Introduction to Nouthetic Counseling*. The Jay Adams Library. Grand Rapids: Zondervan, 1970.

Akiyama, Kengo. *The Love of Neighbour in Ancient Judaism: The Reception of Leviticus 19:18 in the Hebrew Bible, the Septuagint, the Book of Jubilees, the Dead Sea Scrolls, and the New Testament*. Ancient Judaism and Early Christianity 105. Leiden: Brill, 2018.

American Psychiatric Association. *Diagnostic and Statistical Manual of Mental Disorders: DSM5-TR*. 5th ed., text revision. Washington, DC: American Psychiatric Association, 2022.

Anderson, Herbert. "The Bible and Pastoral Care." In *The Bible in Pastoral Practice: Readings in the Place and Function of Scripture in the Church*, edited by Paul Ballard and Stephen R. Holmes, 196–211. Using the Bible in Pastoral Practice Series. London: Darton, Longman & Todd, 2005.

Anscombe. G. E. M. *Ethics, Religion, and Politics*. The Collected Philosophical Papers 3. Minneapolis: University of Minnesota Press, 1981.

Aristotle. *The Basic Works of Aristotle*. Edited with an introduction by Richard McKeon. New York: Random House, 1941.

———. *Nichomachean Ethics*. Translated by David Ross. New York: Oxford University Press, 2009.

Astley, Jeff. *Ordinary Theology: Looking, Learning and Listening in Theology*. Explorations in Practical, Pastoral, and Empirical Theology. Aldershot, UK: Ashgate, 2002.

Bailey, Kenneth E. *Paul Through Mediterranean Eyes: Cultural Studies in 1 Corinthians*. London: SPCK, 2011.

Baird, John D., and Charles Ryskamp, eds. *The Poems of William Cowper*. Vol 3. Oxford: Oxford University Press, 1995.

Ballard, Paul H., ed. "The Bible as Pastor." Special issue, *Contact: Practical Theology and Pastoral Care* 150.1 (2006).

———. "The Use of Scripture." In *The Wiley-Blackwell Companion to Practical Theology*, edited by Bonnie J. Miller-McLemore, 163–72. Wiley-Blackwell Companions to Religion. Chichester, UK: Blackwell, 2013.

Ballard, Paul, and Stephen R. Holmes, eds. *The Bible in Pastoral Practice: Readings in the Place and Function of Scripture in the Church*. Using the Bible in Pastoral Practice Series. London: Darton, Longman & Todd, 2005.

———. "General Introduction: The Underlying Issues, Challenges and Possibilities." In *The Bible in Pastoral Practice: Readings in the Place and Function of Scripture in the Church*, edited by Paul Ballard and Stephen R. Holmes, xiii–xxiii. Using the Bible in Pastoral Practice Series. London: Darton, Longman & Todd, 2005.

Balthasar, Hans Urs von. *Prayer*. Translated by Graham Harrison. San Francisco: Ignatius, 1986.

Barclay, John M. G. "Faith and Self-Detachment from Cultural Norms: A Study in Romans 14–15." *ZNW* 104 (2013) 192–208.

———. *Paul and the Gift*. Grand Rapids: Eerdmans, 2015.

Bartel, Mark "What Is Spiritual? What Is Spiritual Suffering?" *Journal of Pastoral Care and Counselling* 58.3 (2004) 187–201.

Barth, Karl *Church Dogmatics* II/2, *The Doctrine of God, Part 2*. Edited by G. W. Bromiley and T. F. Torrance. Translated by G. W. Bromiley. Edinburgh: T. & T. Clark, 1957.

Bartholomew, Craig. "In Front of the Text: The Quest of Hermeneutics." In *The Bible in Pastoral Practice: Readings in the Place and Function of Scripture in the Church*, edited by Paul Ballard and Stephen R. Holmes, 135–52. Using the Bible in Pastoral Practice Series. London: Darton, Longman & Todd, 2005.

Bauckham, Richard, and Trevor Hart. *Hope against Hope: Christian Eschatology in Contemporary Context*. Trinity & Truth Series. London: Darton, Longman & Todd, 1999.

Beattie, Melody. *Codependent No More: How to Stop Controlling Others and Start Caring for Yourself*. 2nd ed. Center City, MN: Hazelden, 1987.

Beck Aaron T., et al., eds. *Cognitive Therapy of Depression*. Guilford Clinical Psychology and Psychotherapy Series. New York: Guilford, 1979.

Beker, J. Christiaan. *Suffering and Hope: The Biblical Vision and the Human Predicament*. Philadelphia: Fortress, 1987.

Bellini, Peter J. *The Cerulean Soul: A Relational Theology of Depression*. Studies in Religion, Theology, and Disability. Waco, TX: Baylor University Press, 2021.

Bennett, Zoë. *Using the Bible in Practical Theology*. Explorations in Practical, Pastoral, and Empirical Theology. Burlington, VT: Ashgate, 2013.

Bennet, Zoë, and Christopher Rowland. *In a Glass Darkly: The Bible, Reflection and Everyday Life*. London: SCM 2016.

Bentall, David, and Richard Pilgrim. "The Medicalisation of Misery: A Critical Realist Analysis of the Concept of Depression." *Journal of Mental Health* 8.3 (1999) 261–74.

Bergmann, Michael. "Foundationalism." In *The Oxford Handbook of the Epistemology of Theology*, edited by William J. Abraham and Frederick D. Aquino, 253–73. Oxford Handbooks in Religion and Theology. Oxford: Oxford University Press, 2017.

Biebel, David B., and Harold G. Koenig. *New Light on Depression: Help, Hope & Answers for the Depressed & Those Who Love Them*. Grand Rapids: Zondervan, 2004.

Billman, Kathleen D., and Daniel L. Migliore. *Rachel's Cry: Prayer of Lament and Rebirth of Hope*. 1999. Reprint, Eugene, OR: Wipf & Stock, 2007.

Bird, Michael F., and Preston M. Sprinkle, eds. *The Faith of Jesus Christ: Exegetical, Biblical, and Theological Studies*. Milton Keynes, UK: Paternoster, 2009.

Blazer, Dan G. *The Age of Melancholy: "Major Depression" and Its Social Origins*. New York: Routledge, 2005.

Bloch, Ernst. *The Principle of Hope*. Translated by Neville Plaice et al. Studies in Contemporary German Social Thought. Cambridge: MIT Press, 1986.

Boase, Elizabeth, and Christopher G. Frechette, eds. *Bible Through the Lens of Trauma*. SemeiaSt 86. Atlanta: SBL Press, 2016.

Bondi, Richard. "The Elements of Character." *JRE* 12 (1984) 201–18.

Bonhoeffer, Dietrich. *The Collected Sermons of Dietrich Bonhoeffer: Volume 2*. Edited by Victoria J Barnett. Translated by Claudia D. Bergmann et al. Minneapolis: Fortress, 2017.

Brabham, D Allen. "Pastoral Counseling and the Interpretation of Scripture." In *An Introduction to Pastoral Counseling*, edited by Wayne E. Oates, 222–35. Nashville: Broadman, 1959.

Brampton, Sally. *Shoot the Damn Dog: A Memoir of Depression*. London: Bloomsbury, 2018.

Brawley. Robert L., ed. *Character Ethics and the New Testament: Moral Dimensions of Scripture*. Louisville: Westminster John Knox, 2007.

Bray, Gerald L., ed. and trans. *Romans*. 2nd ed. ACCS. Downers Grove, IL: InterVarsity, 2005.

Briggs, Richard S. "Biblical Hermeneutics and Practical Theology: Method and Truth in Context." *AThR* 97 (2015) 201–17.

———. *The Virtuous Reader: Old Testament Narrative and Interpretive Virtue*. STI. Grand Rapids: Baker Academic, 2010.

Brown, William P., ed. *Character and Scripture: Moral Formation, Community, and Biblical Interpretation*. Grand Rapids: Eerdmans, 2002.

———. Preface to *Character and Scripture: Moral Formation, Community, and Biblical Interpretation*, edited by William P. Brown, xi–xvi. Grand Rapids: Eerdmans, 2002.

Brueggemann, Walter. "The Formfulness of Grief." *Int* 31 (1977) 263–65.

———. *Spirituality of the Psalms*. Minneapolis: Fortress, 2002.

Brunner, Emil. *Faith, Hope, and Love*. The Earl Lectures 1955. London: Lutterworth, 1957.

Buckley, Jenny. *Palliative Care: An Integrated Approach*. Chichester, UK: Wiley, 2008.

Cahill, Lisa Sowle. "Christian Character, Biblical Community, and Human Values." In *Character and Scripture: Moral Formation, Community and Biblical Interpretation*, edited by William P. Brown, 3–17. Grand Rapids: Eerdmans, 2002.

Capps, Donald. *Agents of Hope: A Pastoral Psychology*. 1995. Reprint, Eugene, OR: Wipf & Stock, 2001.

———. *The Decades of Life: A Guide to Human Development*. Louisville: Westminster John Knox, 2008.

———. *Jesus the Village Psychiatrist*. Louisville: Westminster John Knox, 2008.

———. *Still Growing: The Creative Self in Older Adulthood*. Eugene, OR: Cascade Books, 2014.

Carmichael, Liz. *Friendship: Interpreting Christian Love*. London: T. & T. Clark, 2004.

Carroll R., M. Daniel, and Jacqueline E. Lapsley, eds. *Character Ethics and the Old Testament: Moral Dimensions of Scripture*. Louisville: Westminster John Knox, 2007.

Carlson, Dwight L. *Why Do Christians Shoot Their Wounded? Helping (Not Hurting) Those with Emotional Difficulties*. Downers Grove, IL: InterVarsity, 1994.

Carson, Marion L. S. "Deep Heat and Bandages? Historical Criticism, Bounded Indeterminacy, and Pastoral Care." *EvQ* 82 (2010) 340–52.

———. *The Pastoral Care of People with Mental Health Problems*. New Library of Pastoral Care. London: SPCK, 2008.

———. "Sheer Grace: Psalm 88, Depression and the Dark Night of the Spirit." *Communio Viatorum* 59 (2017) 160–76.

Carter, John D. "Adams' Theory of Nouthetic Counselling." *Journal of Psychology and Theology* 3 (1975) 143–55.

Carter, John D., and Bruce Narramore. *The Integration of Psychology and Theology: An Introduction*. Rosemead Psychology Series. Grand Rapids: Zondervan, 1979.

Cartledge, Mark J. "The Use of Scripture in Practical Theology: A Study of Academic Practice." *Practical Theology* 6 (2013) 271–83.

Casey, Nell, ed. *Unholy Ghost: Writers on Depression*. New York: HarperPerennial, 2001.

Cessario, Romanus. *The Moral Virtues and Theological Ethics*. 2nd ed. Notre Dame, IN: University of Notre Dame Press, 2009.

Challis, William. *The Word of Life: Using the Bible in Pastoral Care*. Handbooks of Pastoral Care. London: Pickering, 1997.

Charon, Rita. *Narrative Medicine: Honoring the Stories of Illness*. Oxford: Oxford University Press, 2006.

Cheavens, Jennifer S., and Lorie A. Ritschel. "Hope Theory." In *Handbook of Positive Emotions*, edited by Michelle M. Tugade et al., 396–412. New York: Guildford, 2014.

Chentsova-Dutton, Yulia E., and Jeanne L. Tsai. "Understanding Depression Across Cultural Contexts." In *Handbook of Depression*, edited by Ian H. Gotlib and Constance L. Hammen, 337–54. 3rd ed. New York: Guilford 2014.

———. "Understanding Depression Across Cultures" in *Handbook of Depression*, edited by Ian H. Gotlib and Constance L. Hammen, 363–85. 3rd ed. New York: Guilford, 2014.

Childs, Brevard S. *Biblical Theology of the Old and New Testaments: Theological Reflection on the Christian Bible*. Minneapolis: Fortress, 1992.

Clements, Keith W. *Faith*. London: SCM, 1981.

Clifton-Smith, Gregory. *Performing Pastoral Care: Music as a Framework for Exploring Pastoral Care*. Studies in Religion and Theology. London: Kingsley, 2016.

Clinebell, Howard. *Basic Types of Pastoral Care & Counselling: Resources for the Ministry of Healing and Growth*. Updated and revised by Bridget Clare McKeever. Nashville: Abingdon, 2011.

Cloud, Henry, and John Townsend. *Boundaries: When to Say Yes, How to Say No to Take Control of Your Life*. Updated and expanded ed. Grand Rapids: Zondervan, 2017.

Cobb, John B., Jr., and David J. Lull. *Romans*. Chalice Commentaries for Today. St Louis: Chalice, 2005.

Cole, Allen Hugh, Jr. *Be Not Anxious: Pastoral Care of Disquieted Souls*. Grand Rapids: Eerdmans, 2008.

Collins, Gary R. *Christian Counseling: A Comprehensive Guide*. 3rd ed. Nashville: Nelson, 2007.

Colwell, John E. *Why Have You Forsaken Me? A Personal Reflection on the Experience of Desolation*. Milton Keynes, UK: Paternoster, 2010.

Comte-Sponville, André. *A Short Treatise on the Great Virtues: The Uses of Philosophy in Everyday Life*. Translated from the French by Catherine Temerson. London: Vintage, 2003.

Cook, Christopher C. H., and Isabelle Hamley eds. *The Bible and Mental Health: Towards a Biblical Theology of Mental Health*. London: SCM, 2020.

Cotter, Jim. *Brainsquall: Soundings from a Deep Depression*. Sheffield, UK: Cairns, 1997.

Coyle, Suzanne M. *Uncovering Spiritual Narratives: Using Story in Pastoral Care and Ministry*. Minneapolis: Fortress, 2014.

Crabb, Larry. *Basic Principles of Biblical Counselling: Meeting Counselling Needs Through the Local Church* Grand Rapids: Zondervan, 1975.

———. *Effective Biblical Counseling: A Model for Helping Caring Christians Become Capable Counselors*. Grand Rapids: Zondervan, 1977.

Crafton, Barbara Cawthorne. *Jesus Wept: When Faith and Depression Meet*. 10th ann. ed. Minneapolis: Fortress, 2019.

Crossley, Michele L. *Introducing Narrative Psychology: Self, Trauma and the Construction of Meaning*. Buckingham, UK: Open University Press, 2000.

Crisp, Roger, and Michael Slote, eds. *Virtue Ethics*. Oxford Readings in Philosophy. Oxford: Oxford University Press, 1997.

Culligan, Kevin, OCD. "The Dark Night and Depression." In *Carmelite Prayer: A Tradition for the 21st Century*, edited by Keith J. Egan, TOCarm, 119–38. New York: Paulist, 2003.

Cunningham, David S. *Christian Ethics: The End of the Law*. London: Routledge, 2008.

Daly, Robert W. "Before Depression: The Medieval Vice of Acedia." *Psychiatry* 70 (2007) 30–51.

Dana, Mary Ann McKibben. "Suffering, Endurance, Character, Hope: Romans 5:1–11." *Journal for Preachers* 28 (2005) 33–36.

Das, A. Andrew. *Solving the Romans Debate*. Minneapolis: Fortress 2007.

Davis, Ellen F. "Preserving Virtues: Renewing the Tradition." *Studies in Christian Ethics* 14.2 (2001) 14–22.

DeYoung, Rebecca Konyndyk. "Resistance to the Demands of Love." In *Acedia*, edited by Robert B. Kruschwitz, 11–18. Waco, TX: Center for Christian Ethics at Baylor University, 2013. https://ifl.web.baylor.edu/sites/g/files/ecbvkj771/files/2022-11/AcediaArticleDeYoung.pdf.

Doehring, Carrie. *The Practice of Pastoral Care: A Postmodern Approach*. Louisville: Westminster John Knox, 2015.

Donfried, Karl P., ed. *The Romans Debate*. Rev. and exp. ed. Peabody, MA: Hendrickson, 1991. Reprint, Grand Rapids: Baker Academic, 2011.

Dravecky, Jan, and C. W. Neal. *A Joy I'd Never Known: One Woman's Triumph over Panic Attacks and Depression*. Grand Rapids: Zondervan, 1996.

Dulles, Avery. "Faith and Revelation." In *Systematic Theology*, edited by Francis Schüssler Fiorenza and John Galvin, 1:135–54. 2 vols. Minneapolis: Fortress, 1991.

Dunn, James D. G. *Jesus and the Spirit: A Study of the Religious and Charismatic Experience of Jesus and the First Christians as Reflected in the New Testament*. NTL. London: SCM, 1975.

———. *Romans 1–8*. WBC 38A. Dallas: Word, 1988.

Dunson, Ben C. "Faith in Romans: The Salvation of the Individual or Life in Community?" *JSNT* 34 (2011) 19–46.

Durà-Vilà, Glòria. *Sadness, Depression, and the Dark Night of the Soul: Transcending the Medicalisation of Sadness*. London: Kingsley, 2017.

Earey, Mark. *Worship That Cares: An Introduction to Pastoral Liturgy*. London: SCM, 2012.

Eastman, Susan Grove. "What Did Paul Think God Is Doing in Christian Communities?" In *The New Cambridge Companion to St Paul*, edited by Bruce W. Longenecker, 209–24. Cambridge Companions to Religion. Cambridge: Cambridge University Press, 2020.

Engberg-Pedersen, Troels. *Paul and the Stoics*. Edinburgh: T. & T. Clark, 2000.

Engel, George. "The Clinical Application of the Biopsychosocial Model." *AJP* 137.5 (1980) 535–44.

Entwistle, David N. *Integrative Approaches to Psychology and Christianity: An Introduction to Worldview Issues, Philosophical Foundations, and Models of Integration*. 3rd ed. Eugene, OR: Cascade Books, 2015.

Eshun, Sussie, and Toy Caldwell-Colbert. "Culture and Mood Disorders." In *Culture and Mental Health: Sociocultural Influences, Theory and Practice*, edited by Sussie Eshun and Regan A. R. Gurung, 181–95. Chichester, UK: Blackwell, 2009.

Esler. Philip E. "Social Identity, the Virtues, and the Good Life: A New Approach to Romans 12:1—15:13." *BTB* 33.2 (2003) 51–63.

Everts, J. M. "Hope." In *Dictionary of Paul and His Letters*, edited by Gerald F. Hawthorne et al., 415–17. Leicester, UK: InterVarsity, 1993.

Fee, Gordon D. *God's Empowering Presence: The Holy Spirit in the Letters of Paul*. Peabody, MA: Hendrickson, 1994.

Foote, Philippa. *Virtues and Vices and Other Essays in Moral Philosophy*. Berkeley: University of California Press, 1978.

Ford, David F. *Christian Wisdom: Desiring God and Learning in Love*. Cambridge Studies in Christian Doctrine 16. Cambridge: Cambridge University Press, 2007.

Fowl, Stephen E. *The Story of Christ in the Ethics of Paul: An Analysis of the Function of the Hymnic Material in the Pauline Corpus*. JSNTSup 36 Sheffield, UK: JSOT Press, 1990.

Fowl, Stephen E., and L. Gregory Jones. *Reading in Communion: Scripture and Ethics in Christian Life*. Grand Rapids: Eerdmans, 1991.

Frede, Dorothea. "The Historic Decline of Virtue Ethics." In *The Cambridge Companion to Virtue Ethics*, edited by Daniel C. Russell, 124–49. Cambridge Companions to Philosophy. Cambridge: Cambridge University Press 2013.

Furnish, Victor Paul. *The Love Command in the New Testament*. Nashville: Abingdon, 1972.

———. *Theology and Ethics in Paul*. Nashville: Abingdon, 1968.

Gallagher, Matthew W., and Shane J. Lopez, eds. *The Oxford Handbook of Hope*. Oxford Library of Psychology. New York: Oxford University Press, 2017.

Galloway, Janice. *The Trick Is to Keep Breathing*. London: Vintage 1991.

Gardner W. H., ed. *Poems and Prose of Gerard Manley Hopkins*. Penguin Poets. 1953. Reprint, Penguin Classics. London: Penguin, 1985.

Garland, David E. "Philippians." In *Expositor's Bible Commentary*, Vol. 12, *Ephesians-Philemon*, 175–261. Edited by Tremper Longman III and David E. Garland. Rev. ed. Grand Rapids: Zondervan, 2006.

Gaventa, Beverly Roberts. *Romans: A Commentary*. NTL. Louisville: Westminster John Knox, 2024.

———. *When in Romans: An Invitation to Linger with the Gospel According to Paul*. Theological Explorations for the Church Catholic. Grand Rapids: Baker Academic 2016.

Gerkin, Charles V. *An Introduction to Pastoral Care*. Nashville: Abingdon, 1997.

———. *The Living Human Document: Re-Visioning Pastoral Counseling in a Hermeneutical Mode*. Nashville: Abingdon, 1984.

Gilbert, Binford Winston. *The Pastoral Care of Depression: A Guidebook.* New York: Routledge, 2012.

Gorman, Michael J. *Cruciformity: Paul's Narrative Spirituality of the Cross.* Grand Rapids: Eerdmans, 2001.

———. *Inhabiting the Cruciform God: Kenosis, Justification, and Theosis in Paul's Narrative Theology.* Grand Rapids: Eerdmans, 2009.

———. *Romans: A Theological and Pastoral Commentary.* Grand Rapids: Eerdmans, 2022.

———, ed. *Scripture and Its Interpretation: A Global, Ecumenical Introduction to the Bible.* Grand Rapids: Baker Academic, 2017.

Greene-McCreight, Kathryn. *Darkness Is My Only Companion: A Christian Response to Mental Illness.* Grand Rapids: Brazos, 2006.

Greider, Kathleen J. *Much Madness is Divinest Sense: Wisdom in Memoirs of Soul-Suffering.* Cleveland, OH: Pilgrim, 2007.

Grenz, Stanley J., and John R. Franke. *Beyond Foundationalism: Shaping Theology in a Postmodern Context.* Louisville: Westminster John Knox, 2001.

Groeschel, Benedict J. *Spiritual Passages: The Psychology of Spiritual Development "for Those Who Seek."* New York: Crossroad, 1983.

Gundry-Volf, Judith M. *Paul and Perseverance: Staying in and Falling Away.* WUNT 2.37. Tübingen: Mohr Siebeck, 1990.

Gunton, Colin. "The Church as a School of Virtue? Human Formation in Trinitarian Framework." In *Faithfulness and Fortitude: In Conversation with the Theological Ethics of Stanley Hauerwas*, edited by Mark Thiessen Nation and Samuel Wells, 211–32. Edinburgh: T. & T. Clark, 2000.

Gupta, Nijay K. *Paul and the Language of Faith.* Grand Rapids: Eerdmans, 2020.

Hall, Amy Laura. "Love: A Kinship of Affliction and Redemption." In *The Oxford Handbook of Theological Ethics*, edited by Gilbert Meilaender and William Werpehowski, 307–22. Oxford Handbooks. Oxford: Oxford University Press, 2007.

Harrington, Daniel J., and James F. Keenan. *Paul and Virtue Ethics: Building Bridges Between New Testament Studies and Moral Theology.* Lanham, MD: Rowman & Littlefield, 2010.

Hart, Rona. *Positive Psychology: The Basics.* The Basics. Abingdon, UK: Routledge, 2020.

Hasin, Deborah S., et al. "Epidemiology of Depressive Disorders." In *Textbook of Psychiatric Epidemiology*, edited by Ming T. Tsuang et al, 289–309. 3rd ed. Chichester, UK: Wiley, 2011.

Hauerwas, Stanley. *Character and the Christian Life: A Study in Theological Ethics.* 1975. Reprint, Notre Dame, IN: University of Notre Dame Press, 1994.

———. *A Community of Character: Toward a Constructive Christian Social Ethic.* Notre Dame, IN: University of Notre Dame Press, 1981.

———. *Naming the Silences: God, Medicine, and the Problem of Suffering.* London: Bloomsbury, 2004.

———. *The Peaceable Kingdom: A Primer in Christian Ethics.* Notre Dame, IN: University of Notre Dame Press, 1991.

Hauerwas, Stanley, and Charles Pinches. *Christians Among the Virtues: Theological Conversations with Ancient and Modern Ethics.* Notre Dame: University of Notre Dame Press, 1997.

Hauerwas, Stanley, and William H. Willimon. *Resident Aliens: Life in the Christian Colony.* Nashville: Abingdon, 1989.

Hays, Richard B. *Echoes of Scripture in the Letters of Paul.* New Haven: Yale University Press, 1993.

———. *The Faith of Jesus Christ: The Narrative Substructure of Galatians 3:1—4:11.* 2nd ed. The Biblical Resource Series. Grand Rapids: Eerdmans, 2002.

———. "PISTIS CHRISTOU and Pauline Theology: What Is at Stake?" In *Pauline Theology.* Vol. 4, *Looking Back, Pressing On*, edited by E. Elizabeth Johnson and David M. Hay, 35–60. SymS 4. Atlanta: Scholars, 1997.

Healy, David. *Let Them Eat Prozac: The Unhealthy Relationship Between the Pharmaceutical Industry and Depression.* New York: New York University Press, 2004.

Hebblethwaite, Brian. *The Christian Hope.* Rev. ed. Oxford: Oxford University Press, 2010.

Herdt, Jennifer A. "Frailty, Fragmentation, and Social Dependency in the Cultivation of Christian Virtue." In *Cultivating Virtue: Perspectives from Philosophy, Theology, and Psychology*, edited by Nancy E. Snow, 227–49. New York: Oxford University Press, 2015.

Hibbs, Thomas S. "Interpretations of Aquinas's Ethics Since Vatican II." In *The Ethics of Aquinas*, edited by Steven J. Pope, 412–25. Moral Traditions Series. Washington, DC: Georgetown University Press, 2002.

Hill, Craig C. *In God's Time: The Bible and the Future.* Grand Rapids: Eerdmans, 2002.

Hopkins, Denise Dombkowski, and, Michael S. Koppel, eds. *Grounded in the Living Word: The Old Testament and Pastoral Care Practices.* Grand Rapids: Eerdmans, 2010.

Horrell, David G. *The Bible and the Environment: Towards a Critical Ecological Biblical Theology.* Biblical Challenges in the Contemporary World. Sheffield, UK: Equinox, 2010.

———. *An Introduction to the Study of Paul.* 3rd ed. T. & T. Clark Approaches to Biblical Studies. London: Bloomsbury T. & T. Clark, 2015.

———, ed. *Social-Scientific Approaches to New Testament Interpretation.* London: T. & T. Clark, 1999.

Horwitz, Allan V., and Jerome C. Wakefield. *The Loss of Sadness: How Psychiatry Transformed Normal Sorrow into Depressive Disorder.* New York: Oxford University Press, 2007.

Hulme, William, and Lucy Hulme. *Wrestling with Depression: A Spiritual Guide to Reclaiming Life.* Minneapolis: Augsburg, 1995.

Hunt, Dave. *Beyond Seduction: A Return to Biblical Christianity.* Eugene, OR: Harvest House, 1978.

Hurding, Roger. *Roots and Shoots: A Guide to Counselling and Psychotherapy.* Updated ed. London: Hodder & Stoughton, 2003.

Hursthouse, Rosalind. *On Virtue Ethics.* Oxford: Oxford University Press, 1999.

Jacobs, Michael. *Still Small Voice: A Practical Introduction to Counselling in Pastoral and Other Settings.* New ed. New Library of Pastoral Care. London: SPCK, 1993.

Jervis, L. Ann. *At the Heart of the Gospel: Suffering in the Earliest Christian Message.* Grand Rapids: Eerdmans, 2007.

Jewett, Robert. *Romans: A Commentary.* Assisted by Roy D. Kotansky. Hermeneia. Minneapolis: Fortress, 2007.

John of the Cross, Saint. *The Collected Works of St John of the Cross.* Translated by Kieran Kavanaugh and Otilio Rodriguez. Washington, DC: ICS, 1991.

Jones, L. Gregory. "Formed and Transformed by Scripture: Character, Community, and Authority in Biblical Interpretation." In *Character and Scripture: Moral Formation,*

Community, and Biblical Interpretation, edited by William P. Brown, 18–33. Gramd Rapids: Eerdmans, 2002.

———. *Transformed Judgment: Toward a Trinitarian Account of the Moral Life*. Notre Dame, IN: University of Notre Dame Press, 1990.

Karp, David A. *Speaking of Sadness: Depression, Disconnection, and the Meanings of Illness*. Updated and expanded ed. New York: Oxford University Press, 2017.

Käsemann, Ernst. *Commentary on Romans*. Translated and edited by Geoffrey W. Bromiley. Grand Rapids: Eerdmans, 1980.

Keshgegian, Flora A. *Time for Hope: Practices for Living in Today's World*. New York: Continuum, 2006.

Kelly, Anthony. *Eschatology and Hope*. Theology in Global Perspective. Maryknoll, NY: Orbis, 2006.

Kelly, Ewan. *Personhood and Presence: Self as a Resource for Spiritual and Pastoral Care*. London T. & T. Clark, 2012.

Kennerley, Helen, et al. *An Introduction to Cognitive Behaviour Therapy: Skills and Applications*. 3rd ed. London: Sage, 2017.

Kenyon, Jane. *Collected Poems* St. Paul: Graywolf, 2005.

King, James, and Charles Ryskamp, eds. *The Letters and Prose Writings of William Cowper*. Vol. 2, *Letters 1782–1786*. Oxford: Clarendon, 1981.

Kirsch, Irving. *The Emperor's New Drugs: Exploding the Antidepressant Myth*. London: Bodley Head, 2009.

Knight, Gavin, and Joanna Knight. *Disturbed in Mind and Spirit: Mental Health and Healing in Parish Ministry*. London: Continuum, 2009.

Koenig, Harold G. *Is Religion Good for Your Health? The Effects of Religion on Physical and Mental Health*. Haworth Religion and Mental Health. New York: Haworth, 1997.

Konradt, Matthias. "The Love Command in the Authentic Pauline Letters and Ephesians 5:2: An Intertextual Study in the Development of Agape Ethics in the Pauline Corpus." In *To Recover What Has Been Lost: Essays on Eschatology, Intertextuality and Reception History in Honor of Dale C. Allison Jr.*, edited by Tucker Ferda et al., 214–35. Novum Testamentum Supplements 183. Leiden: Brill, 2020.

Kotrosits, Maia, and Hal Taussig. *Re-reading the Gospel of Mark Amidst Loss and Trauma*. New York: Palgrave Macmillan, 2013.

Kotva, Joseph J., Jr. *The Christian Case for Virtue Ethics*. Moral Traditions & Moral Arguments. Washington, DC: Georgetown University Press, 1996.

Kruse, Colin G. *Paul's Letter to the Romans*. Pillar New Testament Commentary. Grand Rapids: Eerdmans 2012.

Lambert, Heath. *The Biblical Counseling Movement after Adams*. Wheaton, IL: Crossway, 2011.

LaMothe, Ryan. "An Analysis of Acedia." *Pastoral Psychology* 56.1 (2007) 15–30.

Law, Robert J. K., and Malcolm Bowden. *Breakdowns Are Good for You! A Unique Manual for True Biblical Counselling*. Bromley, UK: Sovereign, 1999.

Lawlor, Clark. *From Melancholia to Prozac: A History of Depression*. Oxford: Oxford University Press, 2012.

Lawrence, Louise J. *Bible and Bedlam: Madness, Sanism, and New Testament Interpretation*. LNTS 594. London: T. & T. Clark, 2018.

Lee, Nancy C., and Carleen Mandolfo, eds. *Lamentations in Ancient and Contemporary Cultural Contexts*. SymS 43. Atlanta: SBL, 2008.

Lester, Andrew. *Hope in Pastoral Care and Counseling*. Louisville: Westminster John Knox, 1995.

Lewis, Thomas Griffin. *Finding God: Praying the Psalms in Times of Depression*. Louisville: Westminster John Knox, 2002.

Lloyd-Jones, David Martyn. *Spiritual Depression: Its Causes and Its Cures*. Grand Rapids: Eerdmans, 1965.

Longenecker, Bruce W., ed. *Narrative Dynamics in Paul: A Critical Assessment*. Louisville: Westminster John Knox, 2002.

Lonsdale, David. *Eyes to See, Ears to Hear: An Introduction to Ignatian Spirituality*. Rev. ed. Traditions of Christian Spirituality Series. Maryknoll, NY: Orbis, 2000.

Luther, Martin. *Lectures on Romans*. Edited and translated by Wilhelm Pauck. LCC 15. Philadelphia: Westminster, 1961.

Lyall, David. *The Integrity of Pastoral Care*. New Library of Pastoral Care. London: SPCK 2001.

Lynch, Gordon. *Pastoral Care & Counselling*. Ethics in Practice. London: Sage, 2002.

Lynch, William F. *Images of Hope: Imagination as Healer of the Hopeless*. 1965. Reprint, Notre Dame, IN: University of Notre Dame Press, 1974.

MacArthur, John, and Wayne A. Mack, eds. *Counseling: How to Counsel Biblically*. The John MacArthur Pastor's Library. Nashville: Nelson, 2005.

Macaskill, Grant. *Autism and the Church: Bible, Theology, and Community*. Waco, TX: Baylor University Press, 2019.

———. *The New Testament and Intellectual Humility*. Oxford: Oxford University Press, 2019.

MacIntyre, Alasdair. *After Virtue: A Study in Moral Theory*. 3rd ed. Notre Dame, IN: University of Notre Dame Press, 2007.

Macquarrie, John. *In Search of Humanity: A Theological and Philosophical Approach*. New York: Crossroad, 1983.

Maier, Bryan N., and Philip G. Monroe. "Biblical Hermeneutics and Christian Psychology." In *Care for the Soul: Exploring the Intersection Between Psychology and Theology*, edited by Mark R. McMinn and Timothy R. Phillips, 276–93. Downer's Grove, IL: InterVarsity, 2001.

Mainwaring, Simon. *Mark, Mutuality, and Mental Health: Encounters with Jesus*. SemeiaSt 79. Atlanta: SBL Press, 2014.

Marcel, Gabriel. *Homo Viator: Introduction to a Metaphysic of Hope*. Translated by Emma Craufurd. London: Gollancz, 1951.

———. *Tragic Wisdom and Beyond*. Translated by Stephen Jolin and Peter McCormick. Northwestern University Studies in Phenomenology & Existential Philosophy. Evanston, IL: Northwestern University Press, 1973.

Martin, Adrienne M. *How We Hope: A Moral Psychology*. Princeton: Princeton University Press, 2014.

Martin, Ralph P. "Reconciliation: Romans 5:1–11." In *Romans and the People of God: Essays in Honor of Gordon D. Fee on the Occasion of his 65th Birthday*, edited by Sven K. Soderlund and N. T. Wright, 36–48. Grand Rapids Eerdmans 1999.

Matthews, Iain. *The Impact of God: Soundings from St John of the Cross*. London: Hodder & Stoughton, 1995.

May, Gerald G. *The Dark Night of the Soul: A Psychiatrist Explores the Connection Between Darkness and Spiritual Growth*. San Francisco: HarperSanFrancisco, 2004.

McCarroll, Pamela R. *The End of Hope—The Beginning: Narratives of Hope in the Face of Death and Trauma.* Minneapolis: Fortress, 2014.

McClure, Barbara J. *Moving Beyond Individualism in Pastoral Care and Counselling: Reflections on Theory, Theology and Practice.* Eugene, OR: Cascade Books, 2010.

McMinn, Mark R., and Timothy R. Phillips, eds. *Care for the Soul: Exploring the Intersection of Psychology and Theology.* Downers Grove, IL: InterVarsity 2001.

Means, J. Jeffrey. "Mighty Prophet/Wounded Healer." *Journal of Pastoral Care & Counselling* 56.1 (2002) 41–49.

Meeks, Wayne A. "The Man from Heaven in Paul's Letter to the Philippians." In *In Search of the Early Christians: Selected Essays,* 106–14. Edited by Allen R. Hilton and H. Gregory Snyder. New Haven: Yale University Press, 2008.

Meilaender, Gilbert. *Faith and Faithfulness: Basic Themes in Christian Ethics.* Notre Dame: University of Notre Dame Press, 1991.

———. *The Limits of Love: Some Theological Explorations.* University Park: Pennsylvania State University Press, 1987.

———. *The Theory and Practice of Virtue.* Notre Dame, IN: University of Notre Dame Press, 1984.

Melcher, Sarah, et al., eds. *The Bible and Disability: A Commentary.* Studies in Religion, Theology, and Disability. London: SCM 2018.

Meller, William H., and Robert H. Albers. "Depression." In *Ministry with Persons with Mental Illness and Their Families,* edited by Robert H. Alders et al., 11–32. Minneapolis: Fortress, 2012.

Messer, Neil. *SCM Study Guide to Christian Ethics.* SCM Study Guides. London: SCM, 2006.

Meynell, Mark. *When Darkness Seems My Closest Friend: Reflections on Life and Ministry with Depression.* London: IVP, 2018.

Migliore, Daniel L. *Faith Seeking Understanding: An Introduction to Christian Theology.* 3rd ed. Grand Rapids: Eerdmans, 2014.

Moltmann, Jürgen. *In the End—The Beginning: The Life of Hope.* Translated by Margaret Kohl. London: SCM, 2004.

———. *Theology of Hope: On the Ground and Implications of a Christian Theology.* SCM Classics. London: SCM 1967.

Moo, Douglas J. *The Epistle to the Romans.* NICNT. Grand Rapids: Eerdmans, 1996.

Moriarty, Glendon. *Pastoral Care of Depression: Helping Clients Heal Their Relationship with God.* New York: Routledge, 2012.

Murdoch, Iris. *The Sovereignty of Good.* Routledge Classics. London: Routledge, 2001.

Murphy, Nancey. "Agape and Non-Violence." In *Visions of Agapē: Problems and Possibilities in Human and Divine Love,* edited by Craig A. Boyd, 61–72. Aldershot, UK: Ashgate, 2008.

———. *Beyond Liberalism and Fundamentalism: How Modern and Postmodern Philosophy Set the Theological Agenda.* Rockwell Lecture Series. Valley Forge, PA: Trinity, 1996.

Narramore, Clyde M. *The Psychology of Counseling.* Grand Rapids: Zondervan, 1960.

National Institute for Health and Care Excellence (NICE). "Depression in Adults: Treatment and Management." NICE guideline NG222. June 29, 2022. https://www.nice.org.uk/guidance/ng222.

Nault, Jean-Charles, OSB. *The Noonday Devil: Acedia, the Unnamed Evil of Our Times.* Foreword by Marc Cardinal. Translated by Michael J. Miller. San Francisco: Ignatius, 2015.

Norris, Kathleen. *Acedia & Me: Marriage, Monks, and a Writer's Life*. New York: Riverhead, 2008.

Nouwen, Henri J. M. *The Return of the Prodigal Son: A Story of Homecoming*. London: Darton, Longman & Todd, 1994.

———. *The Wounded Healer: Ministry in Contemporary Society*. London: Darton, Longman & Todd, 2014.

Nygren, Anders. *Agape and Eros*. London: SPCK, 1953.

———. *Commentary on Romans*. 1949. 1972. Reprint, Minneapolis: Augsburg Fortress, 1978.

O'Callaghan, Paul. *Christ Our Hope: An Introduction to Eschatology*. Washington, DC: Catholic University of America Press, 2011.

O'Donovan, Oliver. *Resurrection and Moral Order: An Outline for Evangelical Ethics*. 2nd ed. Leicester, UK: Apollos, 1994.

Oglesby, William B. *Biblical Themes for Pastoral Care*. Nashville: Abingdon, 1980.

Oliver, Gordon. *Holy Bible, Human Bible: Questions Pastoral Practice Must Ask*. Using the Bible in Pastoral Practice. Grand Rapids: Eerdmans, 2006.

Oord, Thomas Jay. *The Nature of Love: A Theology*. St. Louis: Chalice, 2010.

O'Meara, Thomas. "Virtues in the Theology of Thomas Aquinas." *TS* 58 (1997) 254–85.

Oyebode, Femi. "Autobiographical Narrative and Psychiatry." In *Mindreadings: Literature and Psychiatry*, edited by Femi Oyebode, 25–41. London: RCPsych Publications, 2009.

Palmer, Parker J. *Let Your Life Speak: Listening for the Voice of Vocation*. San Francisco: Jossey-Bass, 2000.

Pattison, Stephen. *A Critique of Pastoral Care*. 3rd ed. London: SCM, 2000.

Pattison, Stephen, et al. *Using the Bible in Christian Ministry: A Workbook*. Using the Bible in Pastoral Practice. London: Darton, Longman & Todd, 2007.

Pearce, Michelle. *Cognitive Behavioral Therapy for Christian Clients with Depression: A Practical Tool-Based Primer*. West Conshohocken, PA: Templeton, 2016.

Pembroke, Neil. *Pastoral Care in Worship: Liturgy and Psychology in Dialogue*. London: T. & T. Clark, 2010.

Peteet, John R. *Depression and the Soul: A Guide to Spiritually Integrated Treatment*. New York: Routledge, 2010.

Petersen, Eugene. *A Long Obedience in the Same Direction: Discipleship in an Instant Society*. 20th anniversary ed. Downers Grove, IL: InterVarsity, 2000.

Peterson, Christopher, and Martin E. P. Seligman. *Character Strengths and Virtues: A Handbook and Classification*. New York: Oxford University Press, 2004.

Pieper, Josef. *Faith, Hope, Love*. San Francisco: Ignatius, 1997.

Piper, John. *When the Darkness Will Not Lift: Doing What We Can While We Wait for God—and Joy*. Nottingham, UK: Inter-Varsity, 2007.

Porter, Jean. "Recent Studies on Aquinas's Virtue Ethic: A Review Essay." *JRE* 26 (1998) 189–215.

———. *The Recovery of Virtue: The Relevance of Aquinas for Christian Ethics*. Louisville: Westminster John Knox, 1990.

———. "Virtue." In *The Oxford Handbook of Theological Ethics*, edited by Gilbert Meilaender and William Werpehowski, 205–19. Oxford Handbooks. Oxford: Oxford University Press, 2007.

Powlison, David. *The Biblical Counseling Movement*. Greensboro, NC: New Growth, 2010.

Pruyser, Paul W. "Maintaining Hope in Adversity." *Bulletin of the Menninger Clinic* 51 (1987) 463–74.

Rabens, Volker. *The Holy Spirit and Ethics in Paul: Transformation and Empowering for Religious-Ethical Life*. WUNT 2/283. Tübingen: Mohr Siebeck.

———. "Indicative and Imperative as the Substructure of Paul's Theology-and-Ethics in Galatians? A Discussion of Divine and Human Agency in Paul." In *Galatians and Christian Theology: Justification, the Gospel, and Ethics in Paul's Letter*, edited by Mark W. Elliott et al, 285–305. Grand Rapids: Baker Academic, 2014.

Radden, Jennifer, and John Z. Sadler. *The Virtuous Psychiatrist: Character Ethics in Psychiatric Practice*. International Perspectives in Philosophy and Psychiatry. Oxford: Oxford University Press, 2009.

Ratcliffe, Matthew. *Experiences of Depression: A Study in Phenomenology*. International Perspectives in Philosophy and Psychiatry. Oxford: Oxford University Press, 2015.

Ricoeur, Paul. "Biblical Hermeneutics." *Semeia* 4 (1975) 27–148.

Rogerson, John. "The Gifts and Challenges of Historical and Literary Criticism." In *The Bible in Pastoral Practice: Readings in the Place and Function of Scripture in the Church*, edited by Paul Ballard and Stephen R. Holmes, 121–34. Using the Bible in Pastoral Practice Series. London: Darton, Longman & Todd, 2005.

Russell, Daniel C., ed. *The Cambridge Companion to Virtue Ethics*. Cambridge Companions to Philosophy. Cambridge: Cambridge University Press, 2013.

———. "Introduction: Virtue Ethics in Modern Moral Philosophy." In *The Cambridge Companion to Virtue Ethics*, edited by Daniel C. Russell, 1–6. Cambridge Companions to Philosophy. Cambridge: Cambridge University Press, 2013.

Sain, Barbara K. "One Body, One Spirit, One Hope: Theological Resources for Those who Struggle to Hope." *Pro Ecclesia* 24 (2015) 197–215.

Sarbin, Theodore R., ed. *Narrative Psychology: The Storied Nature of Human Conduct*. New York: Praeger 1986.

Scheib, Karen D. "Love as a Starting Point for Pastoral Theological Reflection." *Pastoral Psychology* 63 (2014) 705–17.

———. *Pastoral Care: Telling the Stories of Our Lives*. Nashville: Abingdon, 2016.

Schumacher, Bernard N. "Is There Still Hope for Hope?" In *Hope: Claremont Studies in the Philosophy of Religion, Conference 2014*, edited by Ingolf U. Dalferth and Marlene A. Block, 199–226. Religion in Philosophy and Theology 84. Tübingen: Mohr Siebeck, 2016.

Scioli, Anthony, and Henry B. Biller. *Hope in the Age of Anxiety*. New York: Oxford University Press, 2009.

Scrutton, Tasia. *Christianity and Depression: Interpretation, Meaning and the Shaping of Experience*. London: SCM 2020.

Segal, Zindel V. J., et al. *Mindfulness-Based Cognitive Therapy for Depression*. 2nd ed. New York: Guilford, 2013.

Seligman, Martin E. P. *Flourish: A Visionary New Understanding of Happiness and Well-Being*. New York: Free Press, 2011.

———. *Helplessness: On Depression, Development and Death*. Series of Books in Psychology. San Francisco: Freeman 1975.

———. "Positive Psychology, Positive Prevention, and Positive Therapy." In *Handbook of Positive Psychology*, edited by C. R. Snyder and Shane J. Lopez, 3–9. Oxford: Oxford University Press, 2002.

Shields, Harry, and Gary J. Bredfeldt. *Caring for Souls: Counselling Under the Authority of Scripture*. Chicago: Moody Press, 2001.

Schultz, Richard. "Responsible Hermeneutics for Wisdom Literature." In *Care for the Soul: Exploring the Intersection Between Psychology and Theology*, edited by Mark R. McMinn and Timothy R. Phillips, 254–75. Downers Grove, IL: InterVarsity, 2001.

Söding, Thomas. *Das Liebesgebot bei Paulus: Die Mahnung zur Agape im Rahmen der paulinischen Ethik*. NTABh, n.s. 26. Munster: Aschendorff, 1995.

Solomon, Andrew. *The Noonday Demon: An Anatomy of Depression*. London: Vintage, 2002.

Spicq, Ceslaus. *Agapē in the New Testament*. Vol. 2, *Agapē in the Epistles of Paul, the Acts of the Apostles, and the Epistles of St James, St Peter and St Jude*. Translated by Sister Marie Aquinas McNamara, OP, and Sister Mary Honoria Richter, OP. 1965. Reprint, Eugene, OR: Wipf & Stock, 2006.

Stanford, Matthew S. *Grace for the Afflicted: A Clinical and Biblical Perspective on Mental Illness*. Rev. and exp. ed. Downers Grove, IL: IVP Books, 2017.

Stauffer, Ethelbert. "*Agapaō* . . ." In *TDNT*, 1:21–55. Grand Rapids: Eerdmans 1964.

Stendahl, Krister. *Paul Among Jews and Gentiles, and Other Essays*. Philadelphia: Fortress, 1976.

Still, Todd D. *Conflict in Thessalonica: A Pauline Church and Its Neighbours*. JSNTSup 183. Sheffield, UK: Sheffield Academic, 1999.

Strawn, Brent A. *The Bible and the Pursuit of Happiness: What the Old and New Testaments Teach Us About the Good Life*. Oxford: Oxford University Press, 2013.

Styron, William. *Darkness Visible: A Memoir of Madness*. London: Vintage, 2001.

Swinton, John. *Finding Jesus in the Storm: The Spiritual Lives of Christians with Mental Health Challenges*. Grand Rapids: Eerdmans, 2020.

———. *Raging with Compassion: Pastoral Responses to the Problem of Evil*. London: SCM 2018.

———. *Resurrecting the Person: Friendship and the Care of People with Mental Health Problems*. Nashville: Abingdon 2000.

———. *Spirituality and Mental Health Care: Rediscovering a 'Forgotten' Dimension*. Practical Theology Series. London: Kingsley, 2001.

———. "Theology or Therapy? In What Sense Does Depression Exist?" *Philosophy, Psychiatry & Psychology* 22.4 (2015) 295–98.

Sykes, Stephen. "Wonders in the Deep: Cowper, Melancholy and Religion." In *Madness and Creativity in Literature and Culture*, edited by Corinne Saunders and Jane Macnaughton, 104–20. Basingstoke, UK: Palgrave Macmillan, 2005.

Tacchi, Mary Jane, and Jan Scott. *Depression: A Very Short Introduction*. Very Short Introductions. Oxford: Oxford University Press, 2017.

Talbert, Charles H. *Learning Through Suffering: The Educational Value of Suffering in the New Testament and Its Milieu*. Zacchaeus Studies. New Testament. Collegeville, MN: Liturgical, 1991.

Theissen, Gerd. *The Social Setting of Pauline Christianity: Essays on Corinth*. Edited and translated and with an introduction by John H. Schütz. Philadelphia: Fortress, 1982.

Thiselton, Anthony C. *Discovering Romans: Content, Interpretation, Reception*. Discovering Biblical Texts. London: SPCK, 2016.

———. *New Horizons in Hermeneutics: The Theory and Practice of Transforming Biblical Reading*. Grand Rapids: Zondervan, 1992.

Thomas Aquinas, Saint. *Summa Theologica*. Literally translated by Fathers of the English Dominican Province; with synoptical charts. 3 vols. New York: Benzinger, 1947.

Thomas, Robert L. *Evangelical Hermeneutics: The New Versus the Old*. Grand Rapids: Kregel, 2002.

Townsend, Loren. "Pastoral Counseling's History." In *Understanding Pastoral Counseling*, edited by Elizabeth A. Maynard and Jill L. Snodgrass, 17–38. New York: Springer 2015.

Trice, Pamela D., and Jeffrey P. Bjorck. "Pentecostal Perspectives on Causes and Cures of Depression." *Professional Psychology: Research and Practice* 37 (2006) 283–94.

Turner, Denys. *The Darkness of God: Negativity in Christian Mysticism*. Cambridge: Cambridge University Press, 1995.

Van Beek, Aart M. *Cross-Cultural Counseling*. Creative Pastoral Care and Counseling Series. Minneapolis: Fortress, 1996.

Vanstone, W. H. *Love's Endeavour, Love's Expense*. London: Darton, Longman & Todd, 2007.

Wallace, Daniel B. *Greek Grammar Beyond the Basics: An Exegetical Syntax of the New Testament*. Rev. ed. Grand Rapids: Zondervan, 1997.

Wallis, Jim. "The Way of Hope." *Sojourners* July 2, 2015. https://sojo.net/articles/way-hope.

Walls. Jerry L. "The Wisdom of Hope in a Despairing World." In *The Wisdom of the Christian Faith*, edited by Paul Moser and Michael McFall, 244–64. Cambridge: Cambridge University Press, 2012.

Webster, John. "Hope." In *The Oxford Handbook of Theological Ethics*, edited by Gilbert Meilander and William Werpehowski, 291–306. Oxford Handbooks. Oxford: Oxford University Press, 2005.

Westerholm, Stephen. *Understanding Paul: The Early Christian Worldview of the Letter to the Romans*. 2nd ed. Grand Rapids: Baker Academic 2004.

Willard, Dallas. *The Spirit of the Disciplines: Understanding How God Changes Lives*. San Francisco: HarperSanFrancisco, 2009. Epub ed.

Williams, S. Taylor. "Illness Narrative, Depression and Sainthood: An Analysis of the Writings of Mother Theresa." *Journal of Religion and Health* 53 (2014) 290–97.

Wilson, Jonathan R. *Gospel Virtues: Practicing Faith, Hope, and Love in Uncertain Times*. Eugene, OR: Wipf & Stock. 1998.

———. *Living Faithfully in a Fragmented World: From "After Virtue" to a New Monasticism*. 2nd ed. New Monastic Library 6. Eugene, OR: Cascade Books, 2010.

———. *Living Faithfully in a Fragmented World: From "After Virtue" to a New Monasticism*. 2nd ed. New Monastic Library 6. Cambridge: Lutterworth, 2010.

———. "Virtue(s)." In *Dictionary of Scripture and Ethics*, edited by Joel B. Green et al., 1926–30. Grand Rapids: Baker Academic, 2011.

Wimberly, Edward P. *Using Scripture in Pastoral Counseling*. Nashville: Abingdon, 1994.

Winter, Richard. "Jay Adams: Is He Really Biblical Enough?" *Third Way* 5.4 (1982) 9–12.

Wischmeyer, Oda. *Love as Agape: The Early Christian Concept and Modern Discourse*. Translated by Wayne Coppins. Baylor–Mohr Siebeck Studies in Early Christianity. Waco, TX: Baylor University Press. 2021.

Witherington, Ben, III. *Paul's Letter to the Romans: A Socio-Rhetorical Commentary*. With Darlene Hunt. Grand Rapids: Eerdmans 2004.

Wolpert, Lewis. *Malignant Sadness: The Anatomy of Depression*. Rev. ed. with a new introduction. London: Faber & Faber 1999.

World Health Organization. "Depressive Disorder (Depression)." World Health Organization newsroom. Fact sheet published August 29, 2025. https://www.who.int/news-room/fact-sheets/detail/depression.

———. *The ICD-11 International Classification of Diseases: Eleventh Revision*. Geneva: World Health Organization, 2019. https://icd.who.int/browse/2025-01/mms/en.

Wright N. T. *The Letter to the Romans: Introduction, Commentary and Reflections*. In *The New Interpreter's Bible*, edited by Leander E Keck, 10:393–770. 13 vols. Nashville: Abingdon, 2002.

———. "Narrative Theology: The Evangelists' Use of the Old Testament as an Implicit Overarching Narrative." In *Biblical Interpretation and Method: Essays in Honour of John Barton*, edited by Katherine J Dell and Paul M. Joyce, 189–200. Oxford: Oxford University Press 2013.

———. *The New Testament and the People of God*. Christian Origins and the Question of God 1. 1992. Reprint, London: SPCK, 2013.

Wright, Tom. *Surprised by Hope: Rethinking Heaven, the Resurrection, and the Mission of the Church*. London: SPCK, 2007.

Wu, Siu Fung. *Suffering in Romans*. Eugene, OR: Pickwick Publications, 2015.

Wurtzel, Elizabeth. *Prozac Nation: Young and Depressed in America*. New York: Penguin, 1994.

Yanos, Philip T. *Written Off: Mental Health Stigma and the Loss of Human Potential*. Cambridge: Cambridge University Press, 2018.

Yong, Amos. *The Dialogical Spirit: Christian Reason and Theological Method in the Third Millennium* Eugene, OR: Cascade Books, 2014.

———. *The Dialogical Spirit: Christian Reason and Theological Method in the Third Millennium*. Cambridge: Lutterworth, 2014.

Ziesler, John. *Paul's Letter to the Romans*. TPI New Testament Commentaries. London: SCM, 1989.

www.ingramcontent.com/pod-product-compliance
Lightning Source LLC
LaVergne TN
LVHW051000080826
845145LV00009B/2373

* 9 7 8 1 6 6 6 7 5 6 8 3 8 *